The North American Third Edition

Cambridge Latin Course
Unit 2
Teacher's Manual

Revision Editor
Ed Phinney
Chair, Department of Classics & Director, University Foreign Language Resource Center
University of Massachusetts at Amherst, U.S.A.

Consulting Editor
Patricia E. Bell
Teacher of Latin & Assistant Head of Languages
Centennial Collegiate and Vocational Institute, Guelph, Ontario, Canada

Editorial Assistant
Barbara Romaine
Amherst, Massachusetts, U.S.A.

Published by the Press Syndicate of the University of Cambridge
40 West 20th Street, New York, NY 10011-4211, USA

The Cambridge Latin Course was funded and developed by the University of Cambridge School Classics Project and SCDC Publications, London, and is published with the sponsorship of the School Curriculum Development Committee in London and the North American Cambridge Classics Project.

© SCDC Publications 1988

This edition published 1988
Reprinted 1990, 1992, 1998

Printed in the United States of America

ISBN 0-521-34855-2 paperback

CREDITS
The work of the Cambridge School Classics Project is gratefully acknowledged, in particular the editorial skill of Robin Griffin. (See the Introduction to the Unit 1 Teacher's Manual.) The Narrative Points and the plot summaries of the stories in the Stage Commentaries were written expressly for this Manual by William D. Gleason, Latin Teacher at South Hadley (Massachusetts) High School, and Director of the Resource Center, North American Cambridge Classics Project, Amherst, Massachusetts; the Grammatical Points and Sentence Patterns, with Examples, were collected by Patricia E. Bell, Latin Teacher at Centennial Collegiate and Vocational Institute, Guelph, Ontario, and Consulting Editor for the North American Third Edition of the *CLC*.

Contents

Introduction *page*	1
Cultural Content of Unit 2	1
Challenge of Roman Britain and Alexandria	1
Cultural Importance of Roman Britain (Stages 13–16)	2
Cultural Importance of Roman Alexandria (Stages 17–20)	6
Homogeneity of Roman Culture	11
Presentation of Grammar in Unit 2	11
Concessions to the Limitation of Time	12
Correlation of Unit 2 with American National Examinations	13
Audiocassette Recording for Unit 2/Slides and Filmstrip	13
STAGE COMMENTARIES	15
The Language Information Section	94
PART ONE: Review Grammar	95
PART TWO: Reference Grammar	97
PART THREE: Complete Vocabulary	99
Diagnostic Tests	100
Appendix A: Cumulated List of Checklist Words	105
Appendix B: Summary of Changes from the North American Second Edition	110
Bibliography	112

Introduction

Cultural Content of Unit 2

Unit 2 (Stages 13–20) of the Cambridge Latin Course was organized according to the objectives and guidelines described in the Unit 1 Teacher's Manual, pp. 5–6. For direction in overall planning and in selecting methods of presentation, consult the relevant sections in the Unit 1 Teacher's Manual, pp. 8–16. The stage commentaries that follow this introduction will provide further suggestions.

As before, the students' reading material uses, wherever possible, historical characters and situations that illustrate Roman life in the first century A.D. Stages 13–16 are set in Roman Britain, three years after the events of Unit 1. These Stages provide some continuity with Unit 1 through the character of Quintus, son of Caecilius Iucundus. Stages 17–20 are set in Alexandria. The narrative is cast as a flashback in which Quintus describes events that occurred in Alexandria in the period between his escape from Pompeii in A.D. 79 and his arrival in Britain in A.D. 82. Quintus also describes the new life in Alexandria of Clemens, Caecilius' former slave, liberated by Quintus after his father's death.

The rural Romano-British background of Stages 13–16 and the cosmopolitan Alexandrian setting of Stages 17–20, separately, contrast each other and, together, contrast the small-town atmosphere of Pompeii in Unit 1. In some ways, the picture of life in Alexandria foreshadows that of Rome itself, which students will meet in Stage 29 (Unit 3).

The chief characters of Unit 2 are portrayed in fuller detail than are the stereotypes of Unit 1. Quintus and Clemens, carryovers from Unit 1, take on more flesh. The Roman provincial judge Salvius, the Celtic king Cogidubnus, and the rich Roman provincial merchant Barbillus are all three new to Unit 2. These are fully rounded characters from the time they first appear.

Challenge of Roman Britain and Alexandria

The power of the stories in this course to hold students' attention results not only from the interesting personages and plots, but also from the glimpses these provide into their historical and cultural background. While reading the stories, therefore, students, like detectives searching for clues, should always be on the alert for the evidence of Roman life. In

Introduction

Unit 1, students can easily spot allusions to the historical background, because they often know already about Pompeii and its remains.

Unfortunately, however, many North American students (and some teachers) know very little about the Classical remains in southern Britain or in northern Egypt. For one thing, the constructions are not nearly so well preserved as in Pompeii because they were wrecked by raiders or gradually fell into disuse and deteriorated, and much of what had not been destroyed was reused in later constructions. For another thing, most of the remains of the Roman occupation of Britain and Egypt have received less publicity in the North American media by comparison, in Britain, with the monuments of the medieval, Elizabethan, and Georgian periods, and, in Egypt, with the pyramids and richly-decorated tombs of the most ancient pharaohs. Nevertheless, Roman Britain and Egypt are extremely important to the cultural development of Western civilization. Help students develop for these two places mental pictures which are as vivid as their picture of Pompeii.

A fuller picture of life in Roman Britain and Alexandria will emerge from a reading of some of the books listed in the Bibliography, pp. 112–18 below. Details pertinent to the stories are included in the stage commentaries which follow. Here, some general remarks are appropriate.

Cultural Importance of Roman Britain (Stages 13–16)

Because of the colonial origins of Canada and the United States, North American students are likely to be aware of the influence of Great Britain upon their own history and culture. Students may not realize, however, that Britain itself was once a province of the Roman empire (A.D. 43–410).

The indigenous peoples of Britain, various Celtic tribes (see map in Unit 2, p. 38), put up varying degrees of resistance—as did later the North American Indians facing the British and French—to the Latin-speaking Roman invaders. The tribe of Catuvellauni, who lived in the area north of what is now London, was quickly defeated by the Roman army in a decisive battle on the Medway river (in the modern county of Kent, A.D. 43). The Caledonii in what are now called the Highlands of Scotland, though once defeated in a battle with the Romans at Mons Graupius (probably in the modern Grampian region) in A.D. 84, were never assimilated into the Roman province during its 400-year history.

In contrast, a group of Atrebates on the southern Channel coast went over to the Roman conquerors early and quite willingly. The southern Atrebates had already established trading ties with the Romanized Gauls (in modern France) across the Channel and thereby acquired a

Introduction

taste for some of the comforts of the increasingly powerful Mediterranean culture which was then spreading to the farthest parts of Europe. Chief among the imports were wine, jewelry, and vessels made of precious metals, for which the Atrebates traded iron from mines in the southeastern part of their territory, grain, and cattle-hides which Roman soldiers used in large quantities for uniforms and boots. The tribal leaders who controlled trade would soon have learned not only to speak and read the Latin language, but also to shape Latin letters on wooden tablets or stones—a novel procedure for men who probably lacked a writing system for their own Celtic dialect. Some of the wealthier noblemen, in order to learn the Latin language and Roman ways better, would have traveled to Italy and lived there for long periods.

Introduction

People Important to Stories About Roman Britain

Cogidubnus, a tribal leader among the southern Atrebates before the Romans invaded, and later, after A.D. 43, a trusted protégé of the Roman conquerors, is an excellent example of the early Romanized, Latin-speaking Briton. He is a major character in the stories of Unit 2, Stages 13–16 (and Unit 3, Stages 21–28). Some of the details of Cogidubnus' life have been pieced together from the scanty evidence, but his appearance, as shown in the drawings of the students' textbook, is the creation of a modern illustrator's imagination. The articles by Barrett and Bogaers in the journal *Britannia* (see in the Bibliography, p. 112 below) reconstruct, though not without disagreement, the life and politics of this Celtic prince who became a client-king of the Romans. The career of Cogidubnus was complex, but it is clear that he had connections with extremely powerful Romans. Cogidubnus was not just Romanized. He became a citizen-member of the highest, senatorial class of Romans and lived resplendently in their most aristocratic style.

Cogidubnus not only became a client-king, ruling his Celtic people for the benefit of the Romans, but he also seems to have been given a special title, "Great King" (*rēx magnus*), and to have ruled over several tribes that the Roman conquerors had grouped into a single political unit, called the Regnenses or Regni. The form and meaning of their name is disputed; it may mean the People-of-the-Kingdom (*rēgnum*) or it may be a corruption of a Celtic word meaning "stiff-necked" or "proud."

The capital of the Regnenses was Noviomagus, a site now overlaid by the modern city of Chichester (see aerial photograph in students' textbook, p. 57), near the southern coast of Britain. Virtually no remains from the period of Cogidubnus can be seen today, but the medieval walls, substantial parts of which are still standing, follow the line of ancient walls built some time later during the Roman occupation. The important inscription-stone, shown in the photograph and drawing on page 56 of Unit 2 is now built into the wall of the porch on the west side of the Council House, on North Street, in Chichester. The left-hand section of the inscription was never found. The remainder is joined together from four broken pieces and is therefore hard to read. The inscription-stone was originally a single slab of grayish-white Purbeck marble, mined nearby in what is now the county of Dorset. It is this inscription that establishes links between King Cogidubnus and Noviomagus, a cult of Roman instead of Celtic gods, and a "cooperative of workers" (*collēgium fabrōrum*), perhaps the smiths who worked iron from mines on the border of what is now called Kent.

Just over a mile west of Chichester in the village of Fishbourne (on highway A27) a splendid courtyard-centered "palace" (*aula*) was excavated between 1961 and 1968. It is thought that the palace may

have been given to Cogidubnus by the Romans as a reward for his
loyalty, although no direct evidence of Cogidubnus' ownership has yet
been found. Today only a small part of the original palace can be seen
by visitors. A modern building covers the remains of the north wing of
the ancient palace (see groundplan of original palace in Unit 2, p. 74).

No longer visible are the remains of the audience room at the west
side of the palace or the large entrance hall (*ātrium*) facing it across the
courtyard on the east side (see model in Unit 2, p. 73). Remains of the
south wing, which contained the king's living quarters with a view of the
harbor that was then, before it silted up, close by, now lie for the most
part under highway A27. The scale of the palace, however, was
immense; students might want to pace out, on their school field, the
original measurements (see Unit 2, p. 73) in order to get a sense of how
large the palace once was. Only these measurements, the reconstruction
in model-form (filmstrip frame 7; Unit 2, p. 73 and pp. 48–49), or the
photographs of pavement mosaics from the palace (filmstrip frames
10–12; Unit 2, p. 65 bottom) can give us some feeling of the wonder that
this very elaborate Italian-style palace inspired in the king's Celtic
subjects and Roman visitors alike. In fact, the palace at Fishbourne may
have been in its day unparalleled in its magnificence anywhere north of
the Alps:

Salvius, the other major character in the stories of Stages 13–16, was
an Italian-born lawyer and senator whom the emperor appointed
"law-deputy" (*lēgātus iūridicus*) for the province of Britain. Identified as
"circuit judge" on p. 216 of Unit 2 (in the Guide to Characters and
Places), Salvius was required by his office to travel around the province
and preside in various towns over court sessions comprising mostly civil
cases. Because the local people still lived under their own traditional
laws, a legal expert like Salvius was sometimes needed to determine
whether decisions made under native law did or did not conflict with
Roman law. The governor of Britain, however, was himself the final
judge, especially in matters that pertained to Roman citizens. Salvius,
though he was legally subordinate to the governor, reported directly to
the emperor and might easily, in his reports, have misrepresented the
governor's policies and his own activities.

Conspicuous by his absence in Stages 13–16 is the contemporary (the
stories are set in A.D. 82) governor of Britain, Agricola, who was
probably of nobler character than Salvius is shown to be. (Agricola will
appear, conflicting sharply with Salvius, in Unit 3.) Agricola would have
been busy securing the northern borders of the province by fighting
hostile tribesmen. He would have had little time to spend in the
governor's palace in Londinium (modern London) which was then being
built. Salvius would have had freedom, consequently, to do more or less
as he pleased, to travel anywhere in the southern parts of the province,

Introduction

and even to interfere in Cogidubnus' nominally independent management of his own kingdom. The life of Salvius, however, like that of Cogidubnus, is now hard to piece together. His appearance in the illustrations in Stages 13–16, like that of Cogidubnus, reflects the imagination of a modern artist.

The country estate which the authors, in Stages 13–14, have selected as the site of Salvius' home-away-from-Rome is historical, although there is no proof that it belonged to Salvius or that he ever actually lived there. This Roman-style *vīlla* was built on a site in the modern village of Angmering-on-Sea (some 12 miles, 20 kilometers, east of Fishbourne). Angmering is just west of the city of Worthing and a little south of highway A27.

The owner of this estate, as the remains (now re-covered) show, was very wealthy, and he would have had easy access to the Fishbourne palace by the Roman road that underlies much of highway A27.

Cultural Importance of Roman Alexandria (Stages 17–20)

If students know anything at all about the antiquities of Egypt, they are more likely to know about the pyramids at Giza or about King Tutankhamen's fabled tomb in the Valley of the Kings than about Alexandria and its Greek and Roman remains. This Mediterranean seaport city, however, today in Egypt second only to the capital Cairo, was also in antiquity the second most important city of the Roman world. It was founded, in 331 B.C., by the Greek general, Alexander the Great, on the site of an older, native Egyptian village some 12 miles (20 kilometers) west of the Canopic mouth of the Nile river. (This mouth, at the modern town of Abuqir, is now dry.) With the passing years, ruled by the Greek dynasty of Ptolemies, Alexandria became a very large city. Because the city was located at the crossroads of various eastern and western trade routes, it soon grew into an important seaport and trading center, while the population became quite cosmopolitan. Chief among the ethnic mix were Greek immigrants and their descendants; they lived largely in the Greek section in the northern part of the city along the Great Harbor. There was also a large population of Jewish immigrants and their descendants; they lived in the northern section of the city too, but east of the Greeks, near the ancient gate on Canopus Street. A large group of indigenous Egyptians lived in the opposite part of the city, south of the Western Harbor. For locations of these places, see the map of ancient Alexandria in the students' textbook, p. 94, or of modern Alexandria below, p. 9.

When Arab invaders captured Alexandria in A.D. 643, it had already become a minor town. By 1798, when Napoleon's troops landed in Egypt, Alexandria was a mere village, but it began to grow again when in 1820, at the order of the Ottoman governor of Egypt, Muhammad Ali, it was connected by a 45-mile-long (72-km-long) canal to the Nile river and thus given easy access to Cairo. Today Alexandria (called in Arabic "al Iskandariyah"), though more homogeneous in population than in antiquity, is once again a busy, crowded metropolis overlying the ancient foundations. Although the mole which always connected the lighthouse-island with the city has widened from an accumulation of sediment (see aerial photograph of modern Alexandria in students' textbook, p. 93), it still separates the harbor, as the narrower strip did in antiquity, into an eastern and western basin. There is still a lake (now called Lake Maryut) south of the city, but the ancient and wonderful lighthouse (Pharos) to the north of the harbor is gone, although the site is marked by the fortress and mosque built in the fifteenth century A.D. by Sultan Kait Bey, recently restored (see students' textbook, p. 92). Near Abusir, on the coast 27 miles (43 km) west of Alexandria, there is the ruin of a small but ancient lighthouse believed to have belonged to a chain which once stretched from the Pharos at Alexandria westwards to the Greek city of Cyrene (in modern Libya). Near this lighthouse, situated on the same spectacular ridge overlooking the sea, are the ruins of a temple of Osiris.

Ancient Alexandria was famous for the tomb of its founder, Alexander the Great. Remnants of the tomb have not been found, and even its ancient location is unknown. See Fraser I.14–17. Arabic folk-legend, however, locates the tomb beneath the modern mosque of Nebi Danial, the "Prophet Daniel," in the center of the modern city (see map below, p. 9). The legend states that the mummified body of Alexander sits enthroned and crowned in a secret chamber beneath the mosque. But excavations, carried out in the 1920's and 30's below the mosque and in the environs, yielded no such splendid scene. More recent excavations to the southeast of the mosque uncovered in 1963 the remains of a small, well-preserved theater of the later Roman period (see photograph in students' textbook, p. 101).

Alexandria became part of the Roman empire when the first Ptolemy's last ruling descendant, that best known of several Cleopatras in the Ptolemaic line, committed suicide (30 B.C.) rather than march in the triumphal parade of the Roman general Octavian, who later became the Emperor Augustus. The city served as the administrative capital of Egypt during the Roman period. During the early part of this period, Octavian completed the Caesareum, a temple which Cleopatra had begun to honor her lover Antony, but Octavian completed to honor his adoptive father Caesar and himself. This temple stood near the shore in the center of the Great (Eastern) Harbor (see map in students' textbook, p. 94, and Fraser I.24), and it was outside this temple that Quintus and Clemens, newly arrived in Alexandria from Greece, offered their

Introduction

thanksgiving sacrifice. See students' textbook, Stage 17, "Quīntus dē Alexandrīā," p. 79 top.

In front of the Caesareum were erected two obelisks (giant stone needles) which had been brought from the ancient holy city of Heliopolis, where they had stood for many centuries by the temple of the Egyptian god Amon-Re, proclaiming with the hieroglyphs inscribed on their sides the achievements of the Egyptian New Kingdom pharaohs, Thotmes III (1490–1436 B.C.) and Rameses II (1290–1224 B.C.). The Caesareum (with its obelisks), after a checkered history, during which it served as a Christian cathedral, was destroyed in A.D. 912. The obelisks, however, remained standing until A.D. 1303 when one of them fell in an earthquake, and thus they survived—one up, one down—until 1877 when the fallen obelisk was transported to London, where it stands re-erected on the embankment of the Thames river, and until 1879 when the upright one was transported to New York City, where it stands re-erected in Central Park. See photograph in student's textbook, p. 93, and Fraser II.69, fn. 158. This obelisk, now over three-thousand years old, is popularly known (like its counterpart in London) as "Cleopatra's Needle" and is said to be the oldest free-standing man-made artifact in North America. It stands behind the Metropolitan Museum of Art on an east-west axis with the small Egyptian temple from Dendur. This little temple of the Roman period, which shows several reliefs of the Emperor Augustus in the archaic costumes of the Egyptian pharaohs, was dismantled, transported, and rebuilt where it now stands under a glass-and-steel wing on the north side of the Metropolitan Museum. The obelisk, however, is open to the elements, badly corroded by industrial pollutants, and scarred by graffiti—a rather gaunt memorial to the lost glory of Roman imperial Alexandria.

In the southwestern part of the city, in the ancient Egyptian quarter of Alexandria (on an acropolis-like hill now obscured by a rise in the level of the surrounding land), was built the Serapeum, the temple which King Ptolemy III (246–221 B.C.) dedicated to the worship of Alexandria's patron deity, Serapis (see photograph in students' textbook, p. 85 top). The site is still marked by an 84-foot-high (26-meter-high) rose granite column (see photograph in students' textbook, p. 85 bottom). This column was set up, probably about A.D. 297, to honor the Emperor Diocletian, but was later misnamed "Pompey's Pillar" by medieval tourists like the Crusaders who naively assumed that this most visible of Alexandrian landmarks marked the burial-place of the Roman Republican general Pompey, who when defeated by Julius Caesar in 48 B.C. at Pharsala, Greece, fled by ship to Alexandria, only to be assassinated as he stepped unsuspecting from a small fishing boat onto the beach. (For more information on Pompey's career, see C.S.C.P., *Pompey and Caesar*, and especially, on his assassination, pp. 51–54, where

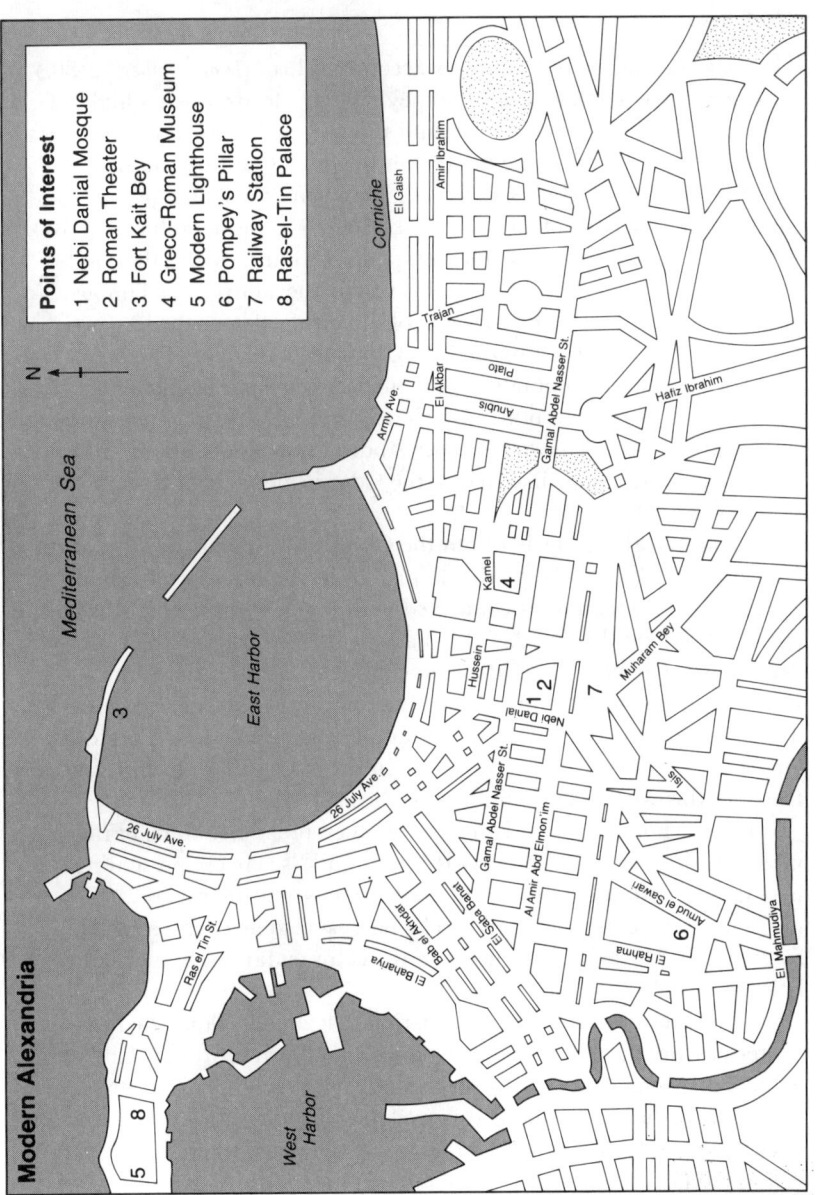

Introduction

there is a translation of Plutarch's account in his *Life of Pompey* 72–80.)

An entrance northwest of "Pompey's Pillar" leads down a flight of stairs into long, ancient underground rooms which may have been part of the Serapeum. It was the Serapeum to which Quintus and his Alexandrian host Barbillus were walking when they met a gabby bore called Plancus (see students' textbook, Stage 17, "ad templum," p. 84). Attached to this temple was the Serapeum Library, the smaller and younger of the two great libraries for which Alexandria was famous. No one knows what happened to the books in either this or the larger Great Library, which was built in the Greek section of the city. The books were probably burned accidentally or on purpose during religious disturbances at the end of the fourth century A.D. Yet the institution of a state library, first known from Alexandria, now flourishes in magnificent collections like that of the Congressional Library, Washington, D.C.

Scholars working, during both the Greek and Roman periods, at the Great Library (students' textbook, p. 156) in the Museum, lived in apartments or dormitories connected with the Museum. This was built by King Ptolemy I (died 284 B.C.) as one of the earliest known "research institutes." The Museum contained, besides the Great Library, study and meeting rooms, botanical and zoological gardens, dining commons, and colonnades that allowed scholars, in a typically Greek way, to stroll, talk, and debate in the open air. Unfortunately, no traces of this complex of buildings have survived.

All the scholars at the Museum were men of letters. Some of them pioneered in a new area of knowledge we call "science," presenting new theorems and hypotheses in mathematics, astronomy, or medicine, particularly anatomy. The names of some of these early scientists at Alexandria are listed in the commentary to Stage 20, p. 92 below.

In the later part of the Roman period, Alexandria flourished as a center of Christian thought. In the fourth and fifth centuries, Christian leaders at Alexandria battled successfully against influential heresies and thus helped shape Christianity as we know it today. Alexandria had long been important to Jews and Christians as the place where in the third century B.C., some seventy anonymous scholars translated into Greek the version of the Old Testament known as the Septuagint Bible. The quotations from the Old Testament in the Greek New Testament were taken from this revered translation.

There are no major historical characters in the stories of Stages 17–20. Young, Pompeian-born Quintus, though historical, may never have actually visited Alexandria. Barbillus, who in our story befriends Quintus, appears on an inscription as an important and influential Roman living in Egypt, but his occupation of merchant and the narrative about him are invented. Other characters in the stories about Alexandria are presented as typical people of that time (A.D. 80–81).

Homogeneity of Roman Culture

Despite the differences in climate, crops, some articles of clothing, and other local variants, life in the Romanized country and town houses was essentially the same in Egypt, in Britain, and everywhere throughout the empire. Although Rufilla, Salvius' wife, served Quīntus, when he was her guest in Britain, a local specialty like oysters (Stage 14: "Quīntus advenit"), or Barbillus, the Alexandrian merchant, took Quīntus, when he was his guest in Egypt, on a trip to hunt Nilotic crocodiles (Stage 19: "vēnātiō"), the daily life in the houses of Barbillus or Salvius was not, for the most part, different from the life we observed, in Unit 1, in the house of the Pompeian banker Caecilius. Very similar would have been the architecture of the houses, the murals painted on the walls, the mosaics on the floors, the red-glazed Samian pottery on the tables, and the jewelry that the women wore. Such uniformity of culture had not existed previously in Europe and the Mediterranean areas, nor would it exist again until modern industrial times.

Presentation of Grammar in Unit 2

Stages 13–16 introduce grammatical items like the infinitive and its uses, complementary (Stage 13) and subjective (Stage 14); the relative clause with nominative or accusative headers (Stage 15); and the forms of the pluperfect tense (Stage 16). Adjectives which in Unit 1 appeared without grammatical comment are now shown, first in Stage 14, to agree with nouns in case and number, and then, in Stage 18, also to agree with nouns in gender.

Stages 17–20 introduce the genitive case into the basic sentence patterns (Stage 17), while the patterns themselves in subsequent stages become more complex and variable in their word order. These stages also introduce the imperative, including negative forms with *nōlī* and *nōlīte*, and the vocative case which so often appears in the context of commands (Stage 19), as well as the present participle in the nominative case (Stage 20). It explicitly discusses the demonstrative pronoun *hic* (Stage 19) and the oblique cases of the determinative pronoun *is* (Stage 20), which students have seen previously several times in their reading.

Unit 2, while introducing new grammatical items, simultaneously reviews and integrates items already met in Unit 1. At the same time, both of these units (1 and 2) themselves become the foundation of Unit 3 yet to come. Make sure that students have assimilated all the

Introduction

grammatical and cultural information presented in the earlier units. For purposes of review, refer students to the Language Information (hereafter LI) Sections of Units 1 and 2. Otherwise, students may not be able to give full attention to the major linguistic advances which lie ahead. In particular, by the end of Stage 20, students should know four tenses (present, imperfect, perfect, and pluperfect) of the four conjugations and four cases (nominative, genitive, dative, and accusative) of the first three declensions.

The Language Information Section for Unit 2, pp. 161–213, contains considerable material for learning and reviewing grammar: (1) a Review Grammar (pp. 162–89) with complete paradigms of old and new forms, brief explanations of major points of grammar with numerous Latin examples, and some manipulation exercises; (2) a Reference Grammar (pp. 190–97) with logical codifications of major points of grammar, list of sentence patterns, and some Latin examples for clarification when necessary. There is also (3) a Complete Vocabulary part (pp. 198–213), where students can find the meanings of Latin words they have forgotten and/or the first three principal parts of Latin verbs they have studied. The Index of Grammatical Topics (pp. 218–19) will also be helpful.

Concessions to the Limitation of Time

If you discover that either the limitation of time or the learning disabilities of students will not allow completion of every story, omit a story here and there rather than omit groups of consecutive stories or, worse, entire stages. Omit any of the following stories when necessary, but when omitting them, be sure to give a brief English summary of their plot to maintain the narrative continuity.

Stage 13 "Salvius fundum īnspicit"
Stage 14 "Rūfilla cubiculum ōrnat" and "Quīntus advenit"
Stage 15 "lūdī fūnebrēs"
Stage 17 "ad templum"
Stage 18 "Clēmēns tabernārius"
Stage 19 "pompa" or "nāvis sacra"
Stage 20 "Petrō" or "fortūna crūdēlis"

Because the study of Roman civilization is such an integral part of the course, be sure to leave some time, even when it is severely limited, for discussion of socio-historical topics. Instead of covering all topics, choose one or two for fairly thorough presentation, e.g. major ones like the administration of the Regnenses' client tribal state by King Cogidubnus or the topography and society of Roman Alexandria.

Introduction

Correlation of Unit 2 with American National Examinations

Many American and Canadian high school students take the Level I National Latin Exam (sponsored by the American Classical League and the National Junior Classical League) in early March of their Latin I year. Since Latin I students using the course will normally have reached the middle of Unit 2 (*c.* Stage 17) by March, they will be quite prepared to succeed on the Level I exam. Because the exam caters to students using many different kinds of textbooks, however, some of the questions will deal with elementary Classical mythology and history of the Roman Republic. If you wish, prepare the students for these questions by assigning them reading in widely available books like Edith Hamilton's *Mythology* and Chester G. Starr's *The Ancient Romans* or any available handbook of mythology and survey of Roman history and civilization. For further information about the National Latin Exam, back copies, and a syllabus, write to A.C.L./N.J.C.L. National Latin Exam, P.O. Box 95, Mt. Vernon, VA 22121.

Many American and Canadian high school students also take a Cambridge Latin Examination (sponsored by the North American Cambridge Classics Project) in the middle and at the end of their Latin I year. Examinations are based on an original passage of facsimile Latin which incorporates the basic grammar, vocabulary, and socio-historical background of each Unit, with questions in two parts, one testing comprehension and grammar; the other, socio-historical background. There are four different examinations, one to follow the conclusion of each of Units 1, 2, 3, and 4, and attractive certificates are awarded to high scorers. A new set of four examinations is available to the teacher for duplication every year in June, and they may be administered at any time during the following school year. For more information about the Cambridge Latin Examination and back copies, write to the Resource Center, North American Cambridge Classics Project (NACCP), Box 932, Amherst, MA 01004–0932.

Audiocassette Recording for Unit 2 / Slides and Filmstrip

Recording

Side 2 of the first of the two C-60 audio-cassettes accompanying the course contains dramatic readings, made by professional actors, of the following stories:

    Stage 13   "trēs servī"
    Stage 14   "Domitilla cubiculum parat"
                 "in tablīnō"

Introduction

    Stage 15   "lūdī fūnebrēs"
    Stage 16   "rēx spectāculum dat"
    Stage 17   "ad templum"
    Stage 18   "prō tabernā Clēmentis"
    Stage 19   "pompa"
    Stage 20   "astrologus victor"

Play one (or part of one) of these dramatizations for the class after the students' second or third reading of the story. Younger students should follow the action and dialogue in their books. Older students might test their aural comprehension by listening only. Students may listen to the cassette on their own Walkmen, or an air band, while miming the actions.

Slides and Filmstrip

Because Unit 2 of the North American Third Edition has been so richly illustrated, no slides or filmstrip have been produced expressly for use with it. In the Stage Commentaries (pp. 15–93 below), however, references have been made to visual material produced for use with the North American Second Edition and British First Edition for the convenience of teachers who own them. The reference "filmstrip" is to the *Cambridge Classical Filmstrip 2: Roman Britain*, accompanying the Second Edition of the Cambridge Latin Course, and the number after it, to the frame within the strip. Information about the frames within the strip is contained in a booklet distributed with the filmstrip. There is no material specifically from Alexandria in *Cambridge Classical Filmstrip 2*, though frame 28 (Isis and Serapis) could be useful. There are also some frames from Alexandria in the *Cambridge Classical Filmstrip 4: Additional Frames*.

The reference "slide" is to the *Cambridge Latin Course Unit II Slides*, and the number after it, to a particular slide. Information about the slides is contained in the First Edition *Unit II Teacher's Handbook*, pp. 20–28.

Stage Commentaries

STAGE 13: IN BRITANNIĀ

BRIEF OUTLINE

Reading passages \} \{Gaius Salvius Liberalis
Background material \{farming and slavery in Roman Britain

Chief grammatical points   infinitive with present tense of *volō* and *possum*
                           -*que*

NARRATIVE POINTS

A.D. Date	Setting	Characters Introduced	Story Line
Autumn 82	Britain: Salvius' country estate	Gaius Salvius Liberalis (circuit judge in southern Britain), Rufilla (Salvius' wife), Varica (farm manager), Philus (accountant), Volubilis (house cook), Bregans (farm slave), Loquax and Anti-Loquax (slave-boys), Pompeius Optatus (mine manager), Alator (mine slave), Cervix (head plowman)	Varica reports that Salvius, who killed a mine slave, has been wounded by the slave's son. Salvius has demanded revenge. At inspection of estate slaves, Salvius strikes Bregans; the dog being led by Bregans attacks Salvius, but cannot be killed because it is a gift from King Cogidubnus. Salvius orders Cervix sold because he is sick.

Stage Commentaries

GRAMMATICAL POINTS

infinitive + *possum, volō, nōlō*; present tense of *possum, volō*
   e.g. *nōs dē hāc coniūrātiōne audīre volumus.*
-que
   e.g. *puerī puellaeque in prīmō ōrdine stābant.*
questions with *nōnne?*
   e.g. *nōnne Cervīx arātōribus praeest?*
perfect passive participle as adjective
   e.g. *dominus est vulnerātus.*
clauses with *ubi* (= "when"), *simulac/simulatque, quamquam*
   e.g. *Bregāns, simulac Salvium vīdit, "domine! domine!" clāmāvit.*
nominative singular of 2nd declension neuter nouns
   e.g. *ubi est vīnum?*
sēcum
   e.g. *Bregāns in mediīs servīs stābat; canem ingentem sēcum habēbat.*
apposition (nominative)
   e.g. *hospes erat Pompēius Optātus, vir benignus.*
nominative predicative adjective
   e.g. *aqua est foeda.*
perfect of *volō*
   e.g. *postrīdiē Salvius fundum īnspicere voluit.*

SENTENCE PATTERNS
(NOM) + INF + V
   e.g. *Volūbilis cēnam optimam coquere potest.*
omission of verb in second of two clauses
   e.g. *ūnus est nocēns, cēterī innocentēs.*

Model Sentences

Gaius Salvius Liberalis is the main character in the stages which deal with Roman Britain (13–16), and he will reappear in Unit 3. The model sentences introduce him and his rural household, together with the new grammatical point; the infinitive with the present tense of *volō* and *possum*. You will find suggestions for presenting and exploring model sentences in the Unit 1 Teacher's Manual, p. 8 and pp. 21–22.

Many students find it easier, at first, to translate *potest* by "is able to," rather than the generally more idiomatic "can," especially since the infinitive is new, but by the end of this stage students should manage both translations, which are highlighted in the first language note, pp. 10–11.

While students are reading the model sentences in Stage 13, encourage comment on the nationality of some of the slaves: Varica

Stage 13

(British and Romanized), Philus (Greek and educated), Volubilis (Egyptian: notice his eyes, drawn in the ancient Egyptian style) and Bregans (British but un-Romanized). Students could also comment on the characteristics of these persons, based on their nationality and education (or lack thereof).

The drawing of an abacus in Philus' hands may intrigue students, since it was the ancient precursor of our own calculator. The counting-board, with its beads and columns for units, tens, hundreds etc. (or monetary equivalents), may strike students as unsophisticated, but the abacus is still widely used in parts of the world, e.g. Japan and Russia.

The following words are new: *cūrat* (new meaning), *potest, fessus, vult, vōcem, suāvem, agilis, saltāre, geminī, nōlunt.*

trēs servī

On a rainy day, three slaves, Philus, Volubilis, and Bregans, are working hard, preparing for the arrival of Salvius. They are all complaining about their life, when Varica, the farm manager bursts in to announce that Salvius is on his way, and is very angry after being wounded by a rebellious slave, while in the region of the Cantiaci. Bregans at once demands that Varica tell the story.

Consult the Unit 1 Teacher's Manual, pp. 8–11, for suggestions on how to handle the reading passages in class.

Younger students might act out this easy story after they have read through it. They should notice the grumbling among the slaves and how this atmosphere of discontent changes to apprehensive excitement at the news of Salvius' injury. The slaves are agog for gossip, but fearful about the consequences of his anger. Ask students what they themselves, if they had been slaves like Philus or Volubilis, would have felt about living and working so far from their native homes. (They might draw analogies with Turks working in Germany or Koreans working in the Arab Gulf states.) The differences between Philus or Volubilis and the Briton Bregans will become clearer in "Bregāns" and "Salvius fundum īnspicit."

Although you will notice the neuter nominative singular *vīnum* (line 6) and the past participle *vulnerātus* (line 13), do not make any special comment. Students will meet more examples of the neuter nominative singular in Stage 18ff., and they can discuss it then. Treat past participles as adjectives until participles are formally discussed in the language notes of Stages 20–22. Students rarely have trouble translating *nōlō* (line 9). If they do, point out that *nōlō* is a short form of *nōn volō*.

The format of the word glossaries in the students' textbook is new, and some students may ask for an explanation. Verbs are now listed as

Stage Commentaries

they occur in the text, but they are followed by the infinitive and the meaning of the infinitive; nouns, as they occur in the text, but followed by the nominative singular form and the meaning of the nominative singular.

The photograph of the Romano-British, sole-ard plow on p. 5 of the students' textbook is reconstructed from wood, with the original metal plowshare. It would have been pulled by a team of oxen, as shown in the bronze statuette on p. 13 of the students' textbook. The plow's knife, or colter, would have made a preliminary vertical cut in the soil ahead of the plowshare. The farmer would have kept the plow on even keel, while it was being pulled, by pushing down on the stilt, or upright portion. For further information about plowing in Roman times, see White 174–78.

coniūrātiō

Varica tells the story of the "conspiracy" of the slaves working in the mine Salvius has been visiting. Salvius, after having a slave executed because he was sick, was subsequently attacked in the night by the slave's son, but escaped with a slight wound, while his attacker was killed by the guards he had initially eluded. Salvius then accused all the slaves of conspiring against him, and demanded they all be executed, but when his host, Pompeius Optatus, objected, satisfied himself with the execution of the guards.

After students have read this story, they might consider its title, pro and con. The title is somewhat ironic, since the conspiracy seems to have existed only in Salvius' imagination. Some students may note that the guards were not likely to have been involved in the plot because they came in and killed Alator before he had a chance to murder Salvius.

The story introduces the character of Salvius. It also puts slavery in a new light, since Salvius treats his slaves very differently from the way Caecilius treated his slaves in Unit 1. Review, in the Unit 1 Teacher's Manual, the commentary on Stage 6 and be prepared to discuss with students the reasons for the differences between Salvius' and Caecilius' treatment of slaves. Be careful to distinguish between the generally humane treatment of slaves (especially if educated) in the *familia urbāna*, and conditions in the *familia rūstica* where slaves were often regarded as animals and worked in chain gangs (see the picture on page 6 of Unit 2, and filmstrip frame 21; slide 41). Life for the slaves in the mines was particularly bad. Many died from overwork or flogging. "Death in their eyes is more to be desired than life, because of the magnitude of the hardships they must bear." (Diodorus V.38; for fuller quotation see Lewis and Reinhold II.158.)

Point out to the students that it was most certainly illegal at this time to execute a slave without trial before a magistrate, but a person of

Stage 13

Salvius' authority could perhaps safely ignore the law in a province remote from Rome. (For legislation governing the treatment of slaves, see Lewis and Reinhold II.268–70.) Nevertheless, what we would regard as cruelty to slaves was not uncommon. Like Salvius, Cato (writing c. 160 B.C.) recommended reducing the rations of sick slaves (*De agri cultura* II.4). The mass execution that Salvius initially demanded recalls Tacitus' description of the over four hundred slaves of Pedanius Secundus executed little more than twenty years before (*Annals* XIV.42–5, translated in C.S.C.P. *The Roman World* Unit II, Item 16b), where treatment of slaves became a matter of public debate, and also recalls the murder of Larcius Macedo by his slaves and the punishment they consequently received (Pliny *Letters* III.14). If there is time, read parts of either story in translation to students (both are in Lewis and Reinhold II.265–6; the one by Pliny is also in Greig's selection, p. 23). Make clear that both incidents were unusual: mass execution of slaves was legal, but the law seems rarely to have been applied. As time went on, treatment of slaves generally became more humane.

Ask the class how they think the slaves would have reacted (1) to the story of Salvius' injury, and (2) to the prospect of Salvius' imminent arrival.

(Note that the Cantiaci are also known in books on Roman Britain as the Cantici or Cantii.)

Bregāns

Varica organizes the slaves for inspection in the courtyard, in anticipation of Salvius' arrival. Bregans stands in their midst with a large dog sent to Salvius by Cogidubnus, a local king. Salvius appears, and proceeds to inspect the slaves; Bregans tries to get Salvius' attention, to show him the dog, but Salvius strikes him for his insolence, and is in turn attacked by the dog. He is only prevented from killing the dog by Bregans' pointed reminder that it was a gift from King Cogidubnus.

This is a straightforward passage designed primarily as a comprehension exercise. The students, individually or divided into groups, can translate the passage among themselves, preferably after you have first read the story aloud. Then the class can answer the questions together. Younger students may also want to dramatize the story, either reading the lines from their books or, if there is time, memorizing them. The characters needed are: a narrator, Varica, Loquax, Anti-Loquax, Bregans, and Salvius. Class members without speaking roles can play horsemen and slaves.

Sometimes students translate *ancillae dominō nostrō cubiculum parant* (line 8) as "The slave girls are preparing our master's bedroom." As students have not yet met the genitive, say that this is "nearly, but not quite

Stage Commentaries

right," and remind them of how they translated, e.g. *Metella filiō dōnum quaerēbat* (in model sentences, Stage 9) or *ego omnibus supplicium poscō* ("coniūrātiō" line 20).

In order to improve students' understanding of verbs, drill the 1st and 2nd persons of the imperfect (introduced in Stage 12) by substituting (e.g. *stābāmus* or *stābās* for *stābant* in line 20 and asking students to translate the new form. (A full description of substitution drills appears in the Unit 1 Teacher's Manual, pp. 11 and 108–9.) Because the story also contains a number of sentences or part-sentences with no nominative stated (e.g. *vīlicus per ōrdinēs ambulābat; servōs īnspiciēbat et numerābat*, lines 5–6), you might also read these aloud and ask for translations, either orally in class or written at home. Include the previous sentence or part-sentence, if the nominative is expressed there.

Question 6 raises the problem of Bregans' character. The story shows him clamoring like a child for attention, but brave (or stupid) enough to talk back to Salvius at the end.

The dog was probably of a breed similar to a modern Irish Wolfhound. The Romans prized British hunting dogs of this breed and imported them into Italy. For details of hunting, see Birley 91–92 and Balsdon 219–20. A picture of a British hunting dog appears in the students' textbook, p. 9.

First Language Note (Infinitive + volō/possum)

After students have read and studied the language note, they should look back at one or more of the stories they have already read, and pick out and translate sentences containing infinitives. In the spare minute or two at the end of the period, ask Latin questions about (e.g.) "trēs servī" like *"quis ad Ītaliam redīre vult?" "quis aquam bibere nōn potest?"* etc. Ask similar questions about the model sentences; then, in order to drill the 1st person singular, ask *"quis saltāre potest?" "quis cantāre potest?" "quis dormīre vult?"* and so on, inviting the respondent to say *"ego saltāre possum"* etc.

Salvius fundum īnspicit

Varica takes Salvius over the farm on a tour of inspection. The harvest is good, but Salvius is displeased with Cervix, the foreman, because he is too sick to work. Salvius orders Varica to sell Cervix, and to withold food from the other plowmen, who also are not working. When Varica explains that a half-collapsed barn is the result of Bregans' carelessness in handling an angry bull, Salvius expresses his contempt for Britons in general, and Bregans in particular.

This is a tour of Salvius' farm, based on Cato's advice to a landowner on how to inspect one's farm in company with the overseer (Cato *De agri*

Stage 13

cultura II; Lewis and Reinhold I.443). Allow students to translate the story either individually at home or together—subdivided into groups or pairs—in class. Then read the story aloud and ask comprehension questions. For example:

> What did Salvius want to do?
> Who took him around the farm?
> What did Varica say about the harvest?
> Where was the grain stored?
> What was the name of the slave in charge of the plowmen?
> Why was he absent?
> What was the effect of his absence?
> When Salvius proposed to get rid of him, what did Varica say in his defense?
> Why did Salvius grudge the plowmen their food?
> What did Salvius see next to the granary?
> Why was it half-ruined?
> Was there a particular reason why Salvius thought Bregans *stultior quam cēterī*?
> What is your impression of Salvius as an estate-owner?

These questions will probably lead to a discussion of Salvius. Students will probably again notice his hard and unsympathetic features, but draw them away from seeing him as a simple stereotype of villainy. He is more complex than that. He is shown here in the role of an estate-owner who, though he employs an overseer for day-to-day supervision, takes a candid interest in its management. He comes in person to see that the estate is being run efficiently and economically. He views the slaves as objects, as factors in the economics of a profitable business, and in so doing he behaves in a way that many Romans would have regarded as normal and acceptable.

Students may also want to talk over Varica's behavior. When Salvius is absent, he takes charge and shows himself capable of making decisions and organizing the work. Now that Salvius is present and demands an accounting, Varica seems lacking in self-confidence, even obsequious. For further details of the job of the *vīlicus* and of farming in general, see C.S.C.P. *The Roman World* Unit II, Book 7: *The Villa*; Lewis and Reinhold I.440–50, II.167–75; Birley 78–99. For further information on villas generally, see Percival. See also filmstrip 5–6; Unit III slides 34–35.

For homework, students might make a list of the slaves who belonged to Salvius, along with their duties. They might prefer to list them in a line of command (Salvius-Varica-Cervix-Bregans and the others), and they might describe analogies with lines of command in modern franchise companies. In class, students might further discuss Salvius' attitude to his slaves and compare it to that of Caecilius in Unit 1 (e.g.

in Stage 6). Particularly, students should look for differences in the treatment of *individual* slaves. In Stage 14, the focus will shift from Salvius' farm slaves to the domestic staff.

In junior high or high school classes, review again complementary infinitives, asking students to spot and translate sentences containing the infinitive + *possum, volō,* or *nōlō*. The perfect tense of *volō* is used here for the first time.

The Soay sheep shown in the photograph on p. 12 are native to the island of Soay (in the St. Kilda group, off the coast of Scotland). These sheep are a variety with short wool, and they show the brown upper parts and white belly of sheep which were kept in Bronze Age Europe. The Soay are a relic breed of the kind of sheep which the Romans might have found when they first settled in Britain. The Romans themselves introduced into Britain their own Mediterranean breeds with longer, finer wool. For further information about Soay sheep, see Frayn 38 and Ryder 116.

Second Language Note (-que)

Younger students often forget *-que*. If this happens, make up further easy sentences containing *et* and then ask students to replace *et* by *-que* in the right position. Use words from the "Words and Phrases Checklist" so that students can simultaneously review basic vocabulary.

Drills

Exercise 1   Type: completion
　　　　　　 Missing item: infinitive
　　　　　　 Test of accuracy: sense

Exercise 2   Type: completion
　　　　　　 Missing item: verb
　　　　　　 Test of accuracy: sense and correct personal ending
　　　　　　 Grammatical point being practiced: 1st, 2nd, and 3rd
　　　　　　　　persons singular of perfect, introduced in Stages 6 and 12
　　　　　　 Incidental practice: clauses with *quod*

Students should complete this second drill orally in class. If they make many mistakes, drill further examples of perfect forms in the singular and ask for translations, e.g. *interfēcit, interfēcī, interfēcistī,* always mixing the order of persons.

When students are doing completion exercises orally, insist they read the correct item in the context of the entire sentence and thus simultaneously practice their pronunciation of Latin.

Stage 13

The Background Material

Divide this material into three reading assignments. Assign the material on Salvius at any time during the stage: that on farming and villas when students are reading "Salvius fundum īnspicit" and that on slaves when they are reading "coniūrātiō."

Salvius

Gaius Salvius Liberalis Nonius Bassus came from a distinguished family in the city of Salvia in the Picenum region of central Italy. Although he may have spent little time there as an adult, he maintained his connections with Salvia by acting as its *patrōnus*.

After he had successfully started his legal career and entered the Senate, Salvius became, at a surprisingly early age, a member of the *Frātrēs Arvālēs*, who were usually all coopted from senatorial families of long standing and had close contact with the emperor, who was always a member. Salvius was obviously destined for power. Before he came to Britain, he was also made a *lēgātus legiōnis* in Moesia (modern Bulgaria and part of Yugoslavia) with the Fifth Legion Macedonica.

For information about Salvius' career in Britain, see Introduction of this Manual, pp. 5–6.

Salvius evidently received a consulship and returned from Britain to Rome by 87. Like many protégés of the Emperor Vespasian, however, he soon fell foul of Vespasian's son and eventual successor, Domitian, and went into exile. He next appears in the records in A.D. 100, under the Emperor Trajan, defending the provincial governor Priscus. Pliny, in his account of the case (*Letters* II.11.17), described him as a sharp, businesslike, energetic, and smooth-tongued speaker. Vespasian earlier had commended him for saying, while defending a rich client, "What is it to Caesar if Hipparchus has a hundred millions?" (Suetonius *Life of Vespasian* 13), thus sidestepping the allegation that Vespasian might wish to have Hipparchus condemned unjustly in order to seize his vast wealth.

Although Salvius had clearly resumed his legal career in Rome, he evidently did not return to political life. When he was offered the governorship of Asia, he declined for reasons unknown.

His full career is outlined in a dedicatory inscription, *C.I.L.* IX, 5533; Dessau 1011. With the abbreviations expanded the inscription reads as follows:

Gaio Salvio, Gaii filio, Velia, Liberali Nonio Basso, consuli, proconsuli provinciae Macedoniae, legato Augustorum, iuridico Britanniae, legato legionis V Macedonicae, fratri Arvali, allecto ab divo Vespasiano et divo Tito inter tribunicios, ab isdem allecto inter praetorios, quinquennali IIII, patrono coloniae. hic sorte proconsul factus provinciae Asiae se excusavit.

Stage Commentaries

To Gaius Salvius Liberalis Nonius Bassus, son of Gaius, of the Velian (voting-tribe), consul, proconsul of the province of Macedonia, imperial legate, chief justice of Britain, legate of the Fifth Legion Macedonica, Arval Brother, promoted to the tribunate by the divine Vespasian and the divine Titus and promoted by the same to the praetorship, a municipal magistrate for twenty years and patron of his town. He obtained by lot the proconsulship of Asia, but excused himself from it.

The gravestone mentioning Rufilla is Dessau 1012 (expanded version):

Vitelliae Gaii filiae Rufillae Gaii Salvi Liberalis consulis, flamini Salutis Augusti, matri optumae, Gaius Salvius Vitellianus vivos.

To Vitellia Rufilla, daughter of Gaius, (the wife) of Gaius Salvius Liberalis the consul, priestess of the Welfare of the Emperor, best of mothers, Gaius Salvius Vitellianus (set this up) in his lifetime.

Here we need not comment further upon Salvius' career, since he will appear again in Units 3 and 4. Students, however, should learn the outline of his life as their first example of the Roman *cursus honōrum* and for later comparison (in Unit 4) with the career of Pliny the Younger. At this point, encourage students to build up a picture of a man in authority, whose character betrays the ruthlessness of a successful politician and the arrogance of a *novus homō*. These traits are particularly evident in his dealings with provincials. But students should not build up too one-sided a picture. The unscrupulousness that they may recognize and condemn in him needs to be balanced against other considerations, and they should discover additional reasons why he might have behaved as he did. A man in Salvius' position and with his responsibilities might have been motivated by genuine fear of a slave-uprising or by fear of the powerful imperial freedmen. In answering to the emperor for his actions, Salvius would have been judged less by moral standards than by his success or failure. After a full discussion, high school students might benefit from writing, as homework, an imaginary dialogue between a friend and an enemy of Salvius. The friend should consider Salvius efficient; the enemy, uncivilized.

Farming in Roman Britain

The villa, see under "Salvius fundum īnspicit," pp. 20–21 above.

The picture on p. 16 of Unit 2 is an aerial photograph. Students should realize that the site is not excavated and that the markings, caused by disturbance of the earth, are only visible, under certain conditions, from the air.

The slaves, see under "coniūrātiō," pp. 18–19 above, and "Salvius fundum īnspicit," pp. 21–22 above.

Words and Phrases Checklist

Explain the new format of these lists to students. 1st and 2nd declension nouns are listed by their nominative singular form; 3rd declension nouns, by their nominative and accusative singular. (Point out to students who have transferred from schools using other textbooks, that the stem of the accusative is the same as that of the genitive.) Verbs are listed by their first three principal parts. Adjectives are listed by their nominative masculine singular form.

Suggestions for Further Work

1 At this stage, students may be eager to write a story, essay, or research paper about Roman slavery. With younger students, the essay might be a description of a day in the ancient mines; the play might be set in a country estate like that described in Stage 13 at Angmering, with slaves from various parts of the empire. To provide inspiration, read selections about clever slaves from a play of Plautus like the *Aulularia* "Pot of Gold," where the slave Pythodicus marshals slaves and supplies for the supposed wedding of the miser Euclio's daughter to his master Megadorus (II.4–9).
2 If you have students living on a farm, they may be enticed to create a slide or slide/tape show for the class on Roman farming using appropriate slides of their own farms complemented by slides of their own drawings of other aspects of Roman farming.

STAGE 14: APUD SALVIUM

BRIEF OUTLINE

Reading passages	daily life in Salvius' villa
Background material	life in Roman Britain (general and historical survey)
Chief grammatical points	agreement of adjective (case and number) imperfect of *possum*

(Note: This stage is quite long. You might consider translating some of the stories aloud yourself (e.g. "Rūfilla," "Domitilla cubiculum parat," "Quīntus advenit," "tripodes argenteī") or summarizing them in English for the students.)

Stage Commentaries

NARRATIVE POINTS

A.D. Date	Setting	Characters Introduced	Story Line
Autumn 82	Britain: Salvius' country estate	Marcia (old slave-woman), Domitilla (slave-girl)	Salvius and Rufilla quarrel over country estate. Domitilla gets Volubilis to do her work. Rufilla uses Salvius' best furnishings to decorate a room for her relative Quintus. Quintus, who came earlier to Britain from Alexandria, has a present for Cogidubnus which is better than Salvius'.

GRAMMATICAL POINTS

increased incidence of attributive adjective: agreement in case and number
    e.g. *amphorae gravēs sunt.*
imperfect of *volō, nōlō, possum*
    e.g. *Marcia urnam vix portāre poterat, quod anus erat.*
subject infinitive + *decōrum, difficile,* etc.
    e.g. *necesse est mihi pavīmentum lavāre.*
vocative in *-ī*
    e.g. *Salvī, audī!*
nōlī
    e.g. *nōlī lacrimāre!*
increased incidence of imperative plural
    e.g. *Loquāx! Anti-Loquāx! portāte hanc amphoram in vīllam!*
present participle
    e.g. *coquus ērubēscēns ad culīnam revēnit.*
ipse
    e.g. *tū ipsa hanc vīllam ēlēgistī.*
apposition (accusative)
    e.g. *mercātōrēs Pompēiānī nōs mīlitēs semper dēcipiēbant.*
accusative predicative adjective
    e.g. *nōs ōrnātrīcēs nihil sordidum facimus.*

SENTENCE PATTERN
decōrum, etc. + *est* + DAT + (ACC) + INF
    e.g. *difficile est mihi magnam amphoram portāre.*

Stage 14

Title Page

Help students with the translation of the title, since *apud* here has a meaning different from the one they met in Stage 13, "among" in the phrase *apud Cantiacōs*. If the students know some French, encourage them to draw an analogy between *apud* and French *chez*.

Model Sentences

Varica orders first Philus, then Loquax and Anti-Loquax, to carry an amphora into the villa. Philus protests that he is too old, the twins that they are only boys, and so cannot do it. In the end, Varica prevails upon Bregans, who complains that amphorae are heavy and difficult to carry, but he is finally obliged to defer to Varica's authority nonetheless.

These illustrate another use of the infinitive: with sentences like *difficile est mihi, necesse est mihi*, etc. Because most students understand this new use easily, you will probably not have to comment further. If students have trouble understanding the infinitive in this construction, either in the model sentences or in the reading passages, provide further examples, e.g.:

difficile est Philō magnam amphoram portāre, quod senex est.
necesse est Bregantī amphorās gravēs portāre.
necesse est vōbīs dīligenter labōrāre.
difficile est mihi librum portāre.

This subjective use of the infinitive will be reviewed in the second language note of Stage 16, together with other uses like the infinitive with *dēbeō*, etc.

These model sentences also drill students in a grammatical construct which has been present in the stories since Stage 3, but not discussed until this stage, viz. agreement of noun and attributive adjective in case and number. You should not, during the students' first reading, discuss noun-adjective agreement. Later, after students have studied the two language notes, they might review the examples of agreement here in the model sentences. (See below, under "Second Language Note.")

The students may identify with Bregans and project the role of Varica onto teachers or parents. You might, however, remonstrate by pointing out that Bregans, though he acts like a child, is a grown man; the reason for his backtalk may have something to do with his total loss of personal freedom. Bregans is at the command, day and night, of Salvius or his agent Varica.

The following words are new: *gravis, necesse*.

Stage Commentaries

Rūfilla

Rufilla accosts Salvius and calls him cruel, because he has brought her to live in a remote country villa, instead of near London, where she has fashionable friends. Salvius objects that she herself chose the house, Rufilla evades his argument, they quibble, and she exits in tears.

This story is quite easy for students to understand; they may want to perform it in class as a play. (Filmstrip 18 will help set the scene, or C.S.C.P. *The Roman World* Unit I, Item 22.) Rufilla, like Metella in Unit 1, is a *mātrōna Rōmāna*, and she bears the responsibility of supervising a large domestic staff. In this story, Rufilla appears somewhat irritable, but living as she does with Salvius, she may have good cause. Salvius, in lines 9–12, seems overeager to put words in her mouth: "*Semprōnia, amīca mea, est fortūnātior quam ego. . . .mihi nihil dās.*"

For the evidence about the historical Rufilla, see Unit 2, Stage 13, p. 15, and this Manual, p. 24 above. To encourage discussion, ask students why Rufilla sends her hairdressers out of the room before she and Salvius argue. What does this action indicate about the status of slaves? Junior high school students, who sometimes know personally what it means to be sent out of the room by parents, may draw analogies between the slaves and themselves!

After the students' first reading, ask them to spot and translate infinitives, review the meaning of *cotīdiē* (so often forgotten), and ask for various kinds of translation for *nōnne*-questions.

There is little archaeological or historical evidence for Roman London at this time, but probably it was already the administrative center of Britain and therefore the likely base for Salvius' legal and political activities. As a major port, London would have been more accessible than the rest of Britain to the Roman culture that Rufilla is said to have missed. Certainly life there would have been livelier than at a *vīlla* like the one excavated at Angmering.

Several of the domestic slaves are named or referred to in this and the following stories. In passing, you might note their various tasks and status.

Domitilla cubiculum parat

Two slave-women have been assigned by Rufilla the task of preparing a bedroom for Rufilla's relative, who will be visiting her. The younger one, Domitilla, petulant at Marcia's insistence that she get to work, plays upon the affection of the cook, Volubilis, who does the work for her, and is rewarded with a kiss.

Students should read this easy story quickly. Subsequent discussion might focus on the character of Domitilla: her complaining, her

Stage 14

awareness of her status as an *ōrnātrīx*, and her ability to manipulate Volubilis the cook.

If you think it advisable, review with students the infinitive, possibly reviewing simultaneously dative endings by changing the persons involved—*necesse est Domitillae cubiculum verrere* instead of *necesse est tibi* . . . (line 8). In line 21 appears the first example of the construction *nōlī* + infinitive, i.e. the negative command. Most students will treat *nōlī* as the equivalent of "don't." If students ask about it, provide the literal translation of *nōlī*, but postpone any fuller discussion until the second language note in Stage 19. By then students will have read examples enough to allow them more fully to understand the explanation. Finally, ask students to comment on the story's title. It is quite ironic.

First Language Note (Adjective Agreement in Case and Number)

Adjectives have been included in the stories from Stage 3 and will rarely cause problems unless you—especially when working with younger students—try to explain too much too soon. The present language note deals with examples of agreement where noun and adjective have similar endings; the next language note, with examples where they have dissimilar endings; and a language note in Stage 18, with agreement in gender. Stay as much as possible with this step-by-step approach.

Ignore the printed instructions in paragraphs 3 and 5 and ask at each sentence a specific question, "*Who* was terrified?" "*Who* was brave?" "*Who* were happy?" etc. This approach presents the noun-adjective relationship in terms of meaning rather than as an abstraction.

After students have studied the language note, ask them to pick out adjectives from stories already read and state the noun each describes. For the present, examples should be restricted to nouns and attributive adjectives of the same declension.

Rūfilla cubiculum ōrnat

Rufilla is pleased with the job the slaves have done in cleaning the bedroom, but feels it still lacks something. Prompted by Domitilla's suggestion, she decides to borrow some of the objects in Salvius' study—a cupboard, a bronze chair, and a gold lampstand—to make the bedroom more attractive.

Adding interest to this story is the ambiguity of the motive behind the slave Domitilla's suggestion that Rufilla have some of the elegant furnishings in Salvius' study moved into the bedroom being prepared for Quintus' arrival. Is Domitilla honestly trying to be helpful, or is she idly making mischief? During discussion, students might consider Domitilla's

Stage Commentaries

previous behavior. How did she, in the story "Domitilla cubiculum parat," justify letting Volubilis do her work for her and clean up the bedroom? In the present story, while talking to the old slave-woman Marcia, did she give Volubilis any credit for the work he had done for her? Did she show any scruple at watching the elderly Marcia scrub the bedroom floor on hands and knees? When reporting to Rufilla, did she give Marcia full credit for scrubbing it? By answering these questions, students will probably find Domitilla somewhat selfish, yet they need to remember that her ordinary household duty was hair-dressing, not room-cleaning: *ego ōrnātrīx sum. . . .nōs ōrnātrīcēs nihil sordidum facimus* ("Domitilla cubiculum parat," lines 12–13).

After students have read the story (twice, if it causes difficulty) and have discussed it, you might also use the story as an occasion for reviewing the perfect tense. Students might spot the perfects, and a volunteer write them on the blackboard. Then you might ask, e.g. "What is the difference in meaning between *optimē labōrāvistī* (line 9) and *bene labōrāvistis* (line 15)?" "If *Domitillam cōnspexit* (line 3) means 'She caught sight of Domitilla' what would *Domitillam cōnspexī* mean?" and "What would be the Latin for 'He caught sight of Domitilla'?" etc.

Younger students might pick out adjectives which have exactly the same endings as their nouns. There are many examples here, including some, like *stulta* (=*Marcia*) in *quam stulta es!* (line 5), which may not be obvious even to older students. Finally, you might want to discuss semantics for a while, helping students explore the difference in meaning between *pūrum* (line 6), where the emphasis is on cleanliness, and *nitidum* (line 16), where the emphasis is on the bright appearance of the freshly scrubbed floor. Students might want to suggest idiomatic translations, like "spotless" for *pūrum*, "shiny" or "glossy" for *nitidum*.

Second Language Note (Adjective Agreement with Different Endings)

After students have studied this note, they might identify the case and number of noun-and-adjective pairs in paragraph 3. Then, after looking back at the model sentences (pp. 22–23) and picking out the adjectives, they might say which nouns these are describing and identify their case and number. For treatment of adjectives generally, see under "First Language Note," above.

in tablīnō

In an encounter in the study between Rufilla and Salvius, who is trying to get some work done, he discovers, to his exasperation, that most of the furnishings are gone from the room. Obliged by this circumstance to

Stage 14

listen to his wife, who is trying to tell him something, he learns, to his further annoyance, that she has invited Quintus, her relative from Pompeii, to visit them. He grumbles about untrustworthy Pompeians, and laments the loss of his cupboard, chair, and lampstand.

To this story have been appended comprehension questions, some of which probe below the surface for interpretation of mood and character. Students with a weak grasp of Latin might need to translate the story before attempting to answer the questions.

When answering question 3, students will undoubtedly observe that Salvius is annoyed by the interruption of his dictation session as well as the loss of his chair and cupboard. He has hardly any good will left to spare when Rufilla announces the impending visit of one of her many distant relatives. Her efforts to explain that the visitor is a nice person of good social standing with an interesting background (he survived the ruin of Pompeii) merely provoke an outburst of prejudice against "Southerners."

This attitude of Salvius may be attributed to his origins. He came from Picenum, a district well to the northeast of Rome, and Picenum had a history of industrial and military power. The lack of sympathy between the north and south of Italy has continued to the present day and reflects in part the different levels of economic development. If the subject is not too controversial, students might discuss similar regional prejudices in North America. How, for example, has the recent industrialization of the American South changed the stereotypes that Yankees used to hold of Southerners? Rufilla, incidentally, exaggerates when she says, *Quīntus vir nōbilis est* (lines 25–26). Quintus' paternal grandfather was a slave. Any noble connections he may have, come through Rufilla herself.

Draw students' attention to *aliquid* (lines 7 and 15), since students often forget it. It recurs in "tripodes argenteī." You might also want to review the translation of *num*-questions like "*num tū sellam et armārium ē tablīnō extrāxistī?*" (line 33). The first example occurred in Stage 11 (see second language note there) and will recur in the second language note of Stage 15.

Drills

Exercise 1   Type: translation
               Grammatical point being practiced: infinitive

Exercise 2   Type: completion
               Missing item: noun
              Test of accuracy: sense and correct case ending
              Grammatical point being practiced: nominative and accusa-
                    tive singular and plural, introduced in Stages 2, 5, and 8

Stage Commentaries

In the second drill, choice of correct noun guarantees the correct choice between singular and plural, but a further choice has to be made between nominative and accusative.

Quīntus advenit

Quintus arrives, and is greeted by Salvius with courtesy if not enthusiasm. Rufilla receives him warmly, with self-deprecating remarks about the humbleness of her hospitality. Salvius attempts to make dinner conversation by inquiring about the disaster at Pompeii, but Rufilla dismisses her husband's remarks as tactless. Salvius contains his anger, apart from a sarcastic remark about the guest bedroom, by which Quintus is visibly impressed.

Despite Salvius' effort (lines 10–11) to turn conversation around to the destruction of Pompeii and Quintus' subsequent adventures, including the reason for his arrival in Britain, he does not here find them out. Quintus describes his adventures later to King Cogidubnus in the penultimate story of Stage 16, "Quīntus dē sē." Since students are almost always eager to know, many of them will be motivated by the suspense to pay attention and read rapidly. They should, in fact, be able to read this story very fast. If they are surprised to find that Salvius is polite, if superficially, to Quintus, remind them that Quintus is the first Roman citizen with whom they have seen Salvius dealing. The etiquette of hospitality was strict in the ancient world. Salvius, though at times ironical, has no difficulty in controlling his feelings.

Some students may be puzzled by *rīsit* (line 5). If so, drill irregular perfects by asking students to look up, in the Complete Vocabulary, pp. 198–213, the perfects of verbs like *agō* and *faciō*, *ostendō* and *respondeō*, *dīcō* and *trahō*, *mittō* and *rīdeō*.

tripodes argenteī

In preparation for a visit to the palace of King Cogidubnus, Quintus casually produces, as gifts, a pair of silver tripods. When Salvius hears of this, he tries to get the better of Quintus by coming up with a more impressive gift, but in the end is obliged to settle for a bronze jug as a present for the king.

This story provides the motive for the journey of Salvius and Quintus to the palace of Cogidubnus in Stage 15. Since the story is fairly easy, students should be able to read it to themselves and then answer, orally, questions like the following:

> What were the slaves doing?
> Who came into the bedroom to talk to Quintus?
> What message did he bring?

What gift did Quintus take from his strong-box and for whom was it intended?
What did Salvius say when he was told of Quintus' gift choice?
Why do you think Salvius said "No" to his steward's first two suggestions?
Why did the steward discourage Salvius from taking the *statua aurāta*?
Recite a translation for the last sentence with an ironic tone of voice suitable to Salvius.
Do you think Salvius had intended to take a present to Cogidubnus at all?
What do you think were Quintus' reasons for offering the king a present?

Students might discuss the worth of each metal object. Cheapest was *aēneus* "made of bronze"—which even the tightfisted Salvius initially rejected. Then came *argenteus* "made of silver"—Quintus' tripods. At the top would have come *aureus* "made of gold." But Salvius preferred to take something *aurātus* "gold-plated," which would have appeared the best, but in fact been of little real value. Discussion of these objects, which were imported together with the wine mentioned in line 22, might lead to further discussion or the assignment of a research paper about the movement of goods in the Roman empire. For further information, consult the commentary to Stage 17, pp. 59, 61, 63 below.

In high schools and colleges where students are studying chemistry, discussion of these objects might lead to further discussion of the abbreviations for many elements; for example, Fe, Ag, Au. Students are always quite excited to learn that these symbols are not just arbitrary.

Do not allow students to assume that a "tripod" was used to hold a photographic camera or such. There is an illustration of two ancient *tripodes* on p. 35 of Unit 2.

Third Language Note (Imperfect of possum)

Students should have no difficulty understanding this note. Drill superior or older students by asking volunteers to transform an imperfect into an infinitive + imperfect of *possum*, e.g.:

servus nōn currēbat.   This becomes: *servus currere nōn poterat.*
ego nōn labōrābam.   This becomes: *ego labōrāre nōn poteram.*

The students should translate both sentences in the pair. If they are unsure of the infinitive forms, they might consult the Complete Vocabulary, pp. 198–213. Further examples:

servus amphoram nōn portābat.   *ancillae nōn saltābant.*
tū nōn dormiēbās.   *nōs nōn currēbāmus.*

Stage Commentaries

The Background Material

Students can be asked to consider the significance for the Romans of the towns marked on the map on p. 38 of Unit 2. The location of minerals will provide a clue for discussion of question 1 below.

The Inscription from Claudius' Arch (C.I.L. 920)

One large and three small fragments, found in the same place, are assumed to belong to the same inscription. (The large piece is shown in the photograph on p. 34 of the Unit 2 Workbook.) These pieces have enabled scholars to make the following conjectural reconstruction.

[ ] = missing part of stone; ( ) = expansion of abbreviation.

TI(BERIO) CLAV[DIO DRVSI F(ILIO) CAI]SARI
    AVGV[STO GERMANI]CO
      PONTIFIC[I MAXIMO TRIB(VNICIA) POTES]TAT(E) XI
COS(VL) V IM[PERATORI XII PATRI PA]TRIAI
SENATVS PO[PVLVSQVE] RO[MANVS Q]VOD
REGES BRIT[ANNIAE] XI [DEVICTOS SINE]
VLLA IACTV[RA IN DEDITIONEM ACCEPERIT]
GENTESQVE B[ARBARAS TRANS OCEANVM]
PRIMVS IN DICI[ONEM POPVLI ROMANI REDEGERIT]

> To the emperor Tiberius Claudius, son of Drusus, Caesar Augustus Germanicus, Pontifex Maximus, holding tribunician power for the eleventh time, Consul for the fifth time, saluted as *Imperātor* twenty-two times, Censor, Father of his Country. The Senate and people of Rome (set this up), because he received the surrender of eleven British kings, who were defeated without any loss and because he was the first to bring barbarian peoples on the other side of the Ocean under Roman rule.

The "eleven British kings" probably included Cogidubnus. See Frere 82ff.

The photograph on p. 40 of the students' textbook shows remains of Watling Street, a Roman road in England, which ran from London northwest to the legionary fortress at Wroxeter. As often happens, a modern road follows closely the line laid out by the Roman army engineers.

Questions for Discussion

1 Why did the Romans want to invade Britain?

2 By what methods, military and otherwise, did they succeed?
3 Why did they find Britain difficult to conquer?
4 What advantages and disadvantages were there in living within the Roman empire?

Further Information on Topics Mentioned in Background Material

1 Caesar's invasion of Britain: *Gallic War* IV.23–V.23. This passage includes a description of the Celtic inhabitants and vague information about geography and mineral resources. Read a translation to the class in order to give an idea of Roman myths and prejudices about Britain. Compare Strabo *Geography* IV.5.2 and 4. See also Webster *Boudica* 34–36.
2 Claudius' invasion: Lewis and Reinhold II.112–13 (from Dio Cassius LX.19–22.1). See also Frere chs. 4 and 5; Scullard 37–39; Webster *The Roman Invasion of Britain*. Ambitious younger students will appreciate Cottrell *The Great Invasion*.
3 Caratacus: Tacitus *Annals* XII.33–40. See also Scullard 39–41; Webster *Rome against Caratacus*.
4 Boudica: Dio Cassius LXII. 1–12; Tacitus *Annals* XIV. 31–37. See also Dudley and Webster; Webster *Boudica*; Andrews. (The name "Boudica," pronounced "Bō deé kah," is similar in meaning to Latin-English "Victoria"; in older English books about Roman Britain it is also spelled "Boudicca," "Boudicea," and "Boadicea." See K. Jackson, "Queen Boudicca?" in the journal *Britannia* X (1979) 255.)
5. Agricola: Tacitus *Agricola*. See also Frere ch. 6.
For further reading on Roman Britain, see in the Bibliography, pp. 112–14 below. For pictures, see filmstrip title-frame and 1–3; slides 52–3.

Suggestions for Further Work

1 Supply junior high or high school students with sources describing Boudica's rebellion in A.D. 61 and perhaps Caesar's description of the Britons. (For details, see list of sources above.) Ask them to write an imaginative account of Boudica's soldiers destroying a Roman estate or the diary of a Roman officer sent against her, with observations about the British natives and how they fight.
2 Show a map of Britain and point out the area that the Romans occupied in the first century A.D., showing the natural boundaries like mountains and rivers that initially deterred their advance. Show the location of Sussex and point out Chichester, near which was built the palace at Fishbourne (filmstrip 7). Show the location of London (filmstrip 4), drawing attention to its location near the estuary of the

Stage Commentaries

Thames river, which facilitated its development as a major port. Show Norfolk, the home of the Iceni tribespeople, whom Boudica, widow of a client-king, led in revolt against the Romans. (Most of these are marked on the map on p. 38 of Unit 2.)

3 The topic of Roman road building is dealt with in Unit 3, Stage 24, in the context of travel in the Roman empire. However, if students show interest here, provide them with information. (Particularly helpful, with a focus on the building of roads in Britain, is Hamey ch. 3.) Ask students to compare ancient with modern road building techniques. Which of the modern types of road, cement or asphalt-topped, most resemble the Roman highways? Which of the highways in North America are best built and most likely to survive (at least in part) as long as some of the Roman roads in Britain? In some cases modern highways in Britain follow the same routes as Roman roads. What kinds of road have North American builders overlaid? (Answer: e.g. Apache Trail, New England cow runs, Oregon Trail, Wells Fargo Pony Express route, etc.)

4 Have students adopt the persona of a patriotic Roman sent to Britain, inclined to be disgruntled but impressed, in spite of himself/herself, by the amenities of life found there. Have each student, using this persona, compose a journal (or compile a slide show) of his/her stay in Britain, illustrating the many aspects of life in Britain that reflect the Roman influence.

STAGE 15: RĒX COGIDUBNUS

BRIEF OUTLINE

Reading passages } { King Cogidubnus
Background material } { the palace at Fishbourne

Chief grammatical points   relative clauses
                           nōnne?

NARRATIVE POINTS

A.D. Date	Setting	Characters Introduced	Story Line
October 13, 82	Britain: Cogidubnus' palace	Cogidubnus (king of the Regnenses), Belimicus (Cantiacan chieftain), Dumnorix (Regnensian chieftain)	Cogidubnus sacrifices to deified Emperor Claudius and cremates his effigy. Boat race between Belimicus and Dumnorix: Belimicus' rashness leads to shipwreck; Dumnorix wins.

GRAMMATICAL POINTS

relative clauses with nominative singular and plural and accusative singular of *quī*
  e.g. *vīnum, quod ancillae ferēbant, erat in paterā aureā.*
infinitive + *dēbeō*
  e.g. *quid facere dēbeō?*

SENTENCE PATTERNS

NOM + Q (relative clause) + V
  e.g. *senex, quī scēptrum tenēbat, erat rēx Cogidubnus.*
omission of verb in first of two clauses
  e.g. *Rēgnēnsēs laetī, Cantiacī miserī erant.*

Model Sentences

These introduce to students Cogidubnus himself (see also the background material in the textbook, the Introduction to this Manual, pp. 4–6 above, and pp. 43–44 below), depicting scenes of tribute offerings made to the king, and of religious sacrifice held at his palace.

The sentence pattern nominative + accusative + verb is now expanded by the addition of a relative clause. Read the sentences aloud with appropriate pauses and word groups. Students rarely have difficulty translating the relative pronoun in these contexts, especially if they know some French and make the association with *qui* and *que*. If they are stymied, allude to the pictures and contextual clues. If, while translating the last three sentences, they render a relative clause as a passive construction (e.g. "The wine, which was being carried by the slave-girls, . . ."), write on the board the clause without the relative pronoun, e.g. *ancillae vīnum ferēbant* for *quae vīnum ferēbant*, and ask for a translation of that before going back to the model sentence and asking for a retranslation of the relative clause.

Unless the students are older or find grammar easy, you should avoid, at this point, explaining the grammar of relative clauses, since several language notes explaining them occur over the next few stages. Again, especially when working with younger students, you should avoid explaining grammatical gender until after it has been explained in Stage 18. If students inquire, explain the two possible meanings of *quod* "that/which" and "because."

Help younger students with terms associated with sacrifice ritual like *patera, lībāvit, āra,* and *sacerdōs* and also describe the practice.

The following words are new (many of them technical terms): *scēptrum, diadēma, rēgīna, maximē, patera, agnum, āram, victima, sacerdōs, bālāvit.*

Associate *bā-lāvit* with the cry of sheep, or students may confuse it with *lībāvit* "poured out."

ad aulam

On the way to the palace, Salvius, with Varica as his agent, forcibly clears the way for himself and his party through a crowd of people who are bound for the same destination. Encountering a broken-down wagon in his path, Salvius has it and its owners thrown into a nearby ditch, when the owners refuse to yield voluntarily.

During the first reading of this story, ask successive students to draw on the blackboard (stick persons will do) the various groups and items mentioned in the first paragraph, thus building up a frieze. Later, review this paragraph by asking students to draw their own illustrative frieze.

The *dignitās*, or "status," of Salvius is revealed in the manner of his progress to the king's palace. Slaves who act as *praecursōrēs* precede his entourage and clear the way of any obstructions. The number of his attendants, the gifts they carry, and the fine horses ridden by Salvius and Quintus are all calculated to impress upon observers his rank, wealth, and importance. During discussion, you might ask students to compare Salvius' outward forms of display with those enacted by public figures today. Ask them, particularly, why horses are still so conspicuous, both in North America and in Britain, during public parades or other official occasions.

Salvius in this story reveals further his attitude toward the provincials, since the young men with the broken wagon are not his slaves, as were the others he treated so contemptuously in Stages 13 and 14. Students might want to discuss the motives behind Salvius' final remark, "*Britannī sunt molestissimī. . . .semper nōs Rōmānōs vexant.*" Are the Britons really such a bother? Is Salvius overly hard-nosed? Is he overwhelmed by the responsibilty of managing a province? In this last case, students should consider exactly what Salvius' responsibility is (see pp. 5–6 and 23–24 above). Perhaps he is arrogating more responsibility than is his.

As work in grammar, you or the students might spot the relative clauses and (if the textbooks are their own!) underline them or color them with a highlighter pen and then retranslate them. Or you might make an enlarged Xeroxed acetate copy of this Latin story and have students come up to the overhead projector to highlight clauses. The visual stimulus of highlighting the clauses is excellent reinforcement here as well as when clausal nesting arrangements become more complex. At this point, however, younger students should not be expected to have grasped the intricacies of the relative pronoun. Unless you have

Stage 15

discussed them previously, you might now discuss the two meanings of *quod*.

sēcum (line 8) occurs here for the first time, but the construction should remind students of *mēcum*, etc. If students do not know pronouns well, review these with them using the Review Grammar, pp. 172–77.

Because the first two paragraphs contain several examples of the imperfect tense, use the few minutes remaining in the period to practice with students the various persons of the imperfect. For example, "If *servus tripodas portābat* means 'A slave was carrying the tripods,' what would *servī tripodas portābant* mean?" Or, "Now look at the first sentence. What did it mean? . . . Now what would be the Latin for 'Quintus was advancing to the palace with many slaves'? And for 'we were advancing'?" And so on. Be sure to ask for variations on *erat* in *magna turba erat in viā* (line 9), e.g. "What would be the Latin for 'Salvius and Quintus were in the street'?"

caerimōnia

Quintus and Salvius enter the palace, to find many British chieftains, as well as many other Romans, awaiting the king's entrance, which follows momentarily. The aged king offers a sacrifice in honor of the Emperor Claudius (now dead nearly thirty years). After the sacrifice, a wax effigy of the emperor is ceremonially burned.

In this story is imagined a ceremony at which Cogidubnus annually honors the memory of his deceased *patrōnus*, the Emperor Claudius. The ceremony is modeled after a description by Herodian (*History* IV.2; Lewis and Reinhold II.565–6) of the ritual that marked the deification of an emperor after his death. This is, of course, a Roman, not a Celtic, ritual, and Cogidubnus, now an old man, observes it with the tenacity of a convert to a new order. Although dignified and venerable, he is now lame and lives on his memories. He does not recognize that with the coming of Salvius his old position and prestige are almost ended.

If students do not know what a "pyre" is, find a volunteer in class who can explain. You may, however, yourself have to explain the significance and mechanics of the eagle "in" the wax effigy. (It was released from a cage in the pyre—directly under the effigy.) When discussing the symbolism of the eagle, American students could draw analogies with the emblematic eagle so often seen on U.S.A. federal buildings and stationery.

Work in grammar should again start with relative clauses. Even younger students should be able to spot them this time before retranslating them. For review, focus on verbs, asking volunteers to substitute tenses across the present, imperfect, and perfect tenses (without changing the person). For example, "In line 30, what does *in*

Stage Commentaries

āreā erat rogus mean? . . . What would *in āreā est rogus* mean?" Or, "What does *prīncipēs ad rogum cum magnā dignitāte prōcessērunt* (lines 30–1) mean? . . . What would be the Latin for 'The chieftains were advancing to the pyre with great dignity'?" And so on. When drilling English to Latin sentences, encourage students to recite complete sentences so that their pronunciation, accent, and grasp of sentence structure may improve too.

If you ask students to transform the last sentence, *animus ad deōs ascendit*, into the present, they will of course find that it stays the same. Ask if they remember other verbs like this, e.g. *contendit*, *ostendit*, and *ruit*, and then review with them the different forms that the perfect tense can take (see the Review Grammar in Unit 1, pp. 206–9). Review of the perfect is well-timed here, since the pluperfect will be introduced in Stage 16.

lūdī fūnebrēs

Funeral games in honor of Claudius are held on the seashore. Many tribes are present, but it is the Cantiaci who win most of the early events. A boat race takes place between the Cantiaci, led by the chieftain Belimicus, and the Regnenses (the king's tribe), led by Dumnorix. Belimicus, eager for victory, carelessly runs his ship up on a reef, whereas the more cautious Dumnorix avoids the reef and wins the race. The Cantiacan sailors must swim for shore, and Belimicus himself is humiliated as he clings to a large rock out at sea.

This boat race is based on Vergil's account of the funeral games celebrated in honor of Anchises, Aeneas' father (*Aeneid* V.114–285). Vergil's games, in turn, are modeled after the Greek chariot races of Homeric funeral games. Boat races were a specifically Roman, not Greek, sport. For many students who tend to associate funerals with droning organ music, you may need to explain that these funeral "games" marked the anniversary of the emperor's death and had political as well as religious significance.

Plan the period for this story carefully. Although it is long and quite difficult because it contains many new words, it will be much more exciting if translated in class at one sitting. If there is a double period available, use it, if possible, for this story. If not, plan as described below.

Start off by reading short portions of text aloud and asking comprehension questions, e.g.:

Who led the procession to the seashore? When?
What did the Britons do there?
Which tribes were present?

Do not, at this point, ask students to translate. Proceed in this manner up to *hoc saxum erat mēta* (line 22).

Stage 15

Here, break off and draw on the board with white chalk a rough sketch of the shore with spectators and, farther off, the turning-point rock. Then ask two students to come up with their books, give one a piece of blue chalk for Belimicus' boat and the other a piece of yellow chalk for Dumnorix's, and ask them to illustrate the progress of the race as it proceeds. Continue the story by asking all students to share the translation, each contributing meanings they know, and monitoring the blue and yellow boats on the board. For homework, assign a written translation of lines 1–22, which were not translated in class.

On the next day, review orally the translation of the entire story and discuss any questions that remain. Encourage idiomatic translations, e.g. *in amīcitiā* (line 3) as "friendly with," "on friendly terms with." As the words appear, write on the board *laetissimī* (line 4), *rōbustissimus* (line 6), *perītissimus* (line 11) and possibly *optimam* and *optimum* (line 20), and then review superlative adjectives by asking students to name the positive (keeping the same number and case), i.e. *laetī, rōbustus, perītus,* and possibly *bonam* and *bonum*. If time allows, point out the comparative *stultior* (line 21) and ask students for the comparative forms of the positives above (again keeping the same number and case), i.e. *laetiōrēs, rōbustior, perītior,* and possibly *meliōrem*. If students cannot do this, lead them systematically through the forms and write them on the board (using only the masculine singular), e.g. *laetus, laetior, laetissimus*. Do not mention comparative adverbs like *celerius* (line 5) unless students ask about them. Finally, you will notice that *Rēgnēnsēs laetī, Cantiacī miserī erant* (lines 44–45) is the first example of a sentence where the first of the two verbs is suppressed (as opposed to double clauses where the second of two verbs is suppressed). Do not comment on the grammar of this sentence, though you may have to help students with the translation. More examples will appear later in Unit 2, and the pattern will be commented on in the Review Grammar, p. 189.

If time is running out, break off the translation review and summarize the rest of the story. Observe the rivalry between the two Celtic chieftains, echoed by their oarsmen and their tribal supporters watching on the shore. Dumnorix and Belimicus have a touchy sense of personal honor; they are quick to mock and take offense. If there is time for discussion, focus on the topic of crowd behavior and the partisanship which, among the proletarian crowds of the large cities and in Rome especially, often erupted into violence. At gladiatorial shows and chariot-races spectators took sides passionately, as at Pompeii in A.D. 59 (see Unit 1 textbook, p. 130). In the Circus Maximus at Rome, troops were kept on duty to put down unruly fans who cheered too violently for their favorites (the charioteers wore tunics with the color of their team: the reds, whites, blues, and greens). Compare modern forms of crowd behavior and the problem of controlling it, for example, at football or ice

Stage Commentaries

hockey matches where the scores are close and the decisions of the referees unpopular. For further details about Roman chariot-racing and seabattles (*naumachiae*), see Balsdon 314–23, 329.

College students, for homework, could write a comparison of this story with its Vergilian model, read first in translation. High school students, for homework, could study for a quiz on the Words and Phrases Checklist in this stage, many of the words of which are included in "lūdī fūnebrēs."

First Language Note (Relative Clauses)

The language note emphasizes the clause rather than the pronoun. It should help students identify relative clauses, translate them appropriately, and identify the noun to which each clause refers. Postpone discussion of the relative pronoun itself until after students have met more examples in their reading, studied gender agreement in Stage 18, and perhaps reviewed the fuller exposition of the relative pronoun in the Review Grammar, p. 175.

After studying this note and picking out the relative clauses in paragraph 3 and translating them, students—should they need more drill—might go back to the model sentences or one of the previous stories and pick out the relative clauses, translate them, and find the noun which each describes. (To older students, you might introduce the word "antecedent.") The clause boundaries will be clearer if students, while reading the Latin sentences aloud, alternate: one group reading in chorus the main clause, another group reading the relative clause.

Drills

Exercise 1 Type: completion
 Missing item: verb
 Test of accuracy: sense and correct ending
 Grammatical point being practiced: present tense of *sum*, introduced in Stages 4, 5, and 10

Exercise 2 Type: completion
 Missing item: noun
 Test of accuracy: correct ending
 Grammatical point being practiced: accusative and dative singular, introduced in Stages 2 and 9; and accusative and dative plural, introduced in Stages 8 and 9

Second Language Note (nōnne?)

nōnne-questions were first introduced in Stage 13; they should cause few problems here. Although students tend to cling to "surely not?" as a translation for *num* and "surely?" for *nōnne*, encourage idiomatic and varied translations, e.g. "You don't mean to tell me that Bregans is working?" Younger students—and older ones too—will benefit from reading the Latin sentences aloud and repeating the English translations in chorus.

The Background Material

The evidence for Cogidubnus' life and career is quite scanty and depends on only two ancient references:

1 Tacitus, *Agricola* 14: *quaedam civitates Cogidumno regi donatae (is ad nostram usque memoriam fidissimus mansit), vetere ac iam pridem recepta populi Romani consuetudine, ut haberet instrumenta servitutis et reges.*

   "Certain territories were given to King Cogidubnus (he remained most loyal right down to our own times) according to an old and long-accepted tradition of the Roman people—using even kings as instruments of slavery."

2 The dedicatory inscription (*R.I.B.* 91) from a temple to Neptune and Minerva at Chichester; see Unit 2 p. 56 and slide 20. The drawing there is based on the following reconstruction.
   [ ] = missing part of stone; ( ) = expansion of abbreviation.

   [N]EPTVNO ET MINERVAE
   TEMPLVM
   [PR]O SALVTE DO[MVS] DIVINAE
   [EX] AVCTORITAT[E TI(BERI)] CLAVD(I)
   [CO]GIDVBNI R[EG(IS) MA]GNI BRIT(ANNORVM)
   [COLLE]GIVM FABROR[VM] ET QVI IN EO
   [SVN]T D(E) S(VO) D(EDERVNT) DONANTE AREAM
   . . .]ENTE PVDENTINI FIL(IO)

   (Note: In the drawing of this inscription in Unit 2, the form COLEGIVM reproduces the presumed original. A letter "E" with a slightly extended foot is a common epigraphical ligature for "LE"; the word therefore can be read as the usual COLLEGIVM.)

   The above version of the partly illegible inscription is based on that of J.E. Bogaers, in *Britannia* X(1979) 243–54. Bogaers rejects the traditional reading of line 5—[CO]GIDVBNI R(EGIS) LEGAT[I] AVG(VSTI) IN BRIT(ANNIA)—which suggests that Cogidubnus was an imperial *lēgātus*, a rank unparalleled for a non-Roman.

Stage Commentaries

Both citations above, particularly the inscription, have been debated by scholars, and their exact meaning, in the absence of further evidence, is likely to remain uncertain.

Cogidubnus' career is likewise very controversial. (See Introduction to this Manual, pp. 4–6; and e.g. Cunliffe *Excavations at Fishbourne*, vol. I.13–14; Barrett.) Little can be stated for certain, but he was possibly educated at Rome and/or controlled the Atrebatic kingdom (roughly modern Sussex and Hampshire) after King Verica fled and before the Emperor Claudius arrived (A.D. 43). Claudius may have rewarded Cogidubnus with the kingdom in return for services rendered during the invasion; Claudius was desperately anxious personally to acquire military prestige and perhaps used the kingship to induce Cogidubnus to help him. The dedication of the Chichester temple to Minerva, goddess of culture, may indicate the considerable progress of Romanization in this client-kingdom. The dedication to Neptune is explained by Chichester's being near the coast of the English Channel.

That Cogidubnus was the owner of Fishbourne is the view of Cunliffe. Students may not follow the chronology of the background section about the palace (last three paragraphs). It refers mainly to the time of the height of Cogidubnus' power, when the palace was built and lived in, but the first and next-to-last paragraphs look back to the earliest years of the conquest. Clarify chronology by showing slides of Fishbourne in chronological sequence (frames 7–13; slides 1–17). For information about the early period of military occupation, see Cunliffe *Fishbourne*, ch. 3. Because granaries are important to the plot of the Modestus stories in Unit 3, mention briefly the evidence for the granary at Fishbourne. It is some closely-set vertical timbers that provided a raised floor to keep grain dry and well ventilated.

If time allows, discuss with students the limitations of evidence on the life of Cogidubnus as an introduction to historiography and the proper use of historical sources. Speculation is a valuable educational exercise, as long as it is based on evidence and the students are conscious that it *is* speculation. A historian sometimes is like a detective. Sometimes he or she must forgo *certain* deductions for those that are *possible* or *probable*. Students too can practice being historians, and you should let them think for themselves and state their views before you intervene or start directing the discussion.

Topics for Discussion

1 Ways in which Cogidubnus might have helped Claudius or Vespasian in A.D. 43 and other methods by which he might have demonstrated his support for Rome.
2 The meaning of the expression "client-king."

3 Ways in which Britain was Romanized.
4 How far the ordinary Regnenses tribespeople supported Cogidubnus in his alliance with the Roman invaders. Might they have seen him as a "collaborator"?

STAGE 16: IN AULĀ

BRIEF OUTLINE

Reading passages } { King Cogidubnus } (continued from
Background material } { the palace at Fishbourne } Stage 15)

Chief grammatical points pluperfect
further uses of the infinitive

NARRATIVE POINTS

A.D. Date	Setting	Characters Introduced	Story Line
Winter 82	Britain: Cogidubnus' palace	Emperor Vespasian	Belimicus tries to get revenge on Dumnorix by introducing a trained bear at a banquet. Bear attacks Cogidubnus; Quintus kills it.
Flashback: Winter 79– Autumn 80	Athens, Alexandria		Quintus tells king his sad story: he sold his father's unburied estates in the winter of 79, visited Athens in the spring and summer of 80, and moved to Alexandria in the autumn of 80. Cogidubnus tells Quintus about his palace: Emperor Vespasian built it in gratitude for the king's help during the Roman invasion of Britain.

GRAMMATICAL POINTS

pluperfect (in relative clause)
    e.g. *in hortō erant multī flōrēs, quōs Cogidubnus ex Ītaliā importāverat.*
increased incidence of infinitive + *decōrum, difficile,* etc.
    e.g. *facile est tibi iocōs facere.*
infinitive + *dēbeō* and *audeō*
    e.g. *sed ursam tractāre nōn audēs!*
relative clauses with accusative plural of *quī*
    e.g. *in aulā erant multae pictūrae, quās pictor Graecus pīnxerat.*

SENTENCE PATTERNS

DAT + ACC + V
    e.g. *ursae cibum et aquam dabat.*
relative clause in sentences with expressed subject omitted
    e.g. *ibi servum, quī tam fortis et tam fidēlis fuerat, līberāvī.*

Model Sentences

Cogidubnus gives Quintus a conducted tour of his palace and stages a banquet for his guests. Emphasize the magnificence of the palace and its Italian style in a non-Italian climate. Encourage students to compare it, say, with the house of the banker Caecilius, illustrated throughout Unit 1, Stage 2. If students find the entertainment bizarre, assure them that it was entirely Romanized: the dancing girl who pops out of the egg and the dwarf jugglers were typical of the entertainers at rich Romans' dinner parties. The students might enjoy looking for further examples in translations of Petronius, *Cena Trimalchionis* 53 ff.; Pliny, *Letters* IX.17.

The new grammatical point, the pluperfect tense, is used only, in this stage, in relative clauses. The context should guide students to the correct translation with "had." Postpone a discussion of the pluperfect forms until after students have read the pertinent language note. Note that the relative clauses now include examples introduced by *quōs* and *quās.*

The following words are new, but their meanings should be clear from the pictures: *fōns, marmoreus, effundēbat, ōvum, saltātrīx, pīlās, iactābant.*

Belimicus ultor

Belimicus, mortified by his defeat in the boat race, decides to take revenge on Dumnorix by exposing him to ridicule. To this end, he secretly works with a she-bear from the king's menagerie, and the bear's trainer, until he feels he can control the animal.

Stage 16

The setback of Belimicus in Stage 15 has an unexpected sequel, which is described in this and the following story. Outraged personal pride drives him to look for means of vengeance, but in the tradition of romantic tales evil plans go wrong and virtue finally triumphs. The events in this and the next story depend closely on the motives of the characters. Focus class discussion on the emotions and thoughts of Belimicus, e.g.:

> How did Belimicus react to his defeat in the boat race?
> Which Latin words and phrases describe his mood?
> What was the attitude of other people towards Belimicus when he was unlucky?
> Why did the Cantiaci make fun of, even insult, their own chieftain? Is this how losers often behave?
> Whom did Belimicus blame for his defeat? Why? (Compare the expression "We was robbed!")
> What do you imagine Belimicus' thoughts and feelings would have been while he was training the bear?

Finally, ask students what they expect Belimicus will do, in the next story, to get his revenge.

The bear in this stage does more than provide story interest; its presence reflects the Roman fondness for exhibiting animals, particularly, though not exclusively, in the amphitheater. Cogidubnus is imagined as owning a miniature zoo of wild animals, cared for by a special slave who would bring them out on occasions like this to show to guests. Trapping these animals in the outlying provinces of the empire and transporting them to Rome was big business. Bears and wolves were imported into Rome from Britain and Germany, lions from North Africa, elephants from East and Central Africa, and crocodiles from the Nile valley. Most of these were targeted for the *vēnātiōnēs*, or sporting hunts, in the amphitheater, whereas a few were sold to wealthy persons who kept them in zoological parks. Ask students to compare the Roman interest in animals with the modern interest in zoos, "safari" parks and tours, and animal films on TV. For more information on the Roman interest in animals, see Balsdon 302ff., Jennison, and Toynbee. Students will enjoy the rather gruesome tale, "Thrasyleon," in C.S.C.P. *The Roman World* Unit I, Book 4: *The Witches of Thessaly*; this is a story from Apuleius *Metamorphoses* 4.13–21, about an unusual private zoo.

For grammatical work, ask students to pick out, translate, and name the antecedent of all the relative clauses. If students—as sometimes happens—translate an accusative relative pronoun, because it heads its clause, as a nominative, write the clause on the board, substituting the accusative of the antecedent for the relative pronoun and then asking the students to translate that before retranslating the relative clause, e.g.

Stage Commentaries

hospitēs rēx ad aulam invītāverat for (*hospitēs*) *quōs rēx ad aulam invītāverat*, or *ursam servus Germānicus custōdiēbat* for (*ursa*) *quam servus Germānicus custōdiēbat*.

Finally, spend part of this and subsequent periods reviewing forms and word order in the LI Section of Unit 2. Because this story contains several examples of the irregular verbs *sum*, *volō*, and *possum*, use it as an occasion to review the material in the Unit 2 Review Grammar, pp. 182–84.

rēx spectāculum dat

At a banquet hosted by the king, Belimicus leads in the she-bear before the astonished guests. Dumnorix, however, is not intimidated, and mocks Belimicus. Belimicus, enraged, shoves the bear at his rival and strikes her, but she turns on him, and then, alarmed by the noise of the spectators, heads directly for the disabled king. Quintus seizes a spear and kills the bear in the nick of time.

This story completes the Belimicus episode. (Belimicus reappears in Stage 24 of Unit 3 where Salvius capitalizes on his hostility towards Dumnorix and Quintus.) Dumnorix taunts Belimicus, who is silent until he is ready to reveal his "secret weapon." Students should, if possible, read the story at one sitting. In order to maintain the pace, translate a few sentences; or, ask comprehension questions about the first half, then—as homework—assign a written or oral translation for the next day's period, when students can discuss details of motive and plot as well as grammatical points. Following are some comprehension questions:

> In the second sentence, why are Salvius and Quintus near the king (lines 1–2)?
> Why do the Romans, not the Britons, show interest in wine?
> Why does Belimicus enter late and sit down in silence?
> How do we know that the bear is well-known before this story starts?
> Why is Belimicus *furēns* (line 31)? Why does the bear turn on him?
> Why does Salvius stand without moving (line 38)?
> Who comes off worst in this story? Best?

At the end of the first long period or during the next day's period, selected students could read through the story as a play. Younger students would enjoy acting out the parts, especially the one playing the bear; a Latin bear *uncat*, or goes "unk unk." The actor playing Belimicus might first rehearse, at the back of the room, Belimicus' *insolēns* speech (lines 25–26), so that he can sound suitably sarcastic when he challenges Dumnorix to handle the bear.

Grammatical practice should again center on relative clauses.

Stage 16

Encourage students at this point to free themselves from over-literal translations, e.g.:

sed ursam, quae saltat, vidēre volō. (lines 13–14)
But I want to see the dancing bear.

ego, quem tū dērīdēs, ursam tractāre audeō. (lines 21–22)
You laugh at me, but I have the nerve to handle the bear.

Then review, with the "Nouns" section of the Review Grammar, pp. 162–66, dative-case endings. For example, in paragraph 5, ask students what would be the singular of the dative *lībertīs* or *cīvibus* (sentence 1) or the plural of the dative *vīlicō* or *agricolae* (sentence 2); or replace datives in the sentences with dative nouns from Appendix A of this Manual, pp. 105–9. If time allows, drill students in verb substitutions, asking them to provide verb forms with different tenses *and* persons, e.g. "If *exspectābat* (line 17) means 'he was waiting for,' what would be the Latin for 'I waited for'?" (Answer: *exspectāvī*) Students may need to consult the Complete Vocabulary, pp. 198–213, to find perfect forms, and students who cannot remember the personal endings, the "Verbs" section of the Review Grammar, pp. 178–81.

Finally, test aural comprehension (see Unit 1 Manual, p. 18) by reading sentences from the "Word Order" section of the Unit 1 Review Grammar, pp. 210–11. This drill will allow students to practice the accusative + verb sentence pattern and thus prepare them for more complex examples of this pattern in the next story (see below under "Quīntus dē sē").

If students raise the question "Who is the more important, Salvius or Cogidubnus?", encourage them to attempt an answer themselves, basing it on what they have read in the stories. By now the distinction between Cogidubnus' titular power and Salvius' real superiority begins to emerge. The students should reserve the final answer to this question, however, until they have read the later developments in Unit 3.

Quīntus dē sē

In a conversation with the king the next day, Quintus reveals that all his family and household, apart from himself and one slave, perished in the destruction of Pompeii. After freeing the slave, Quintus sold his father's property and left Campania, with its sad associations, behind, moving to Athens with the freedman. After a few months, however, Quintus became restless and with the freedman, moved on to Alexandria.

You should be prepared to review Stage 1 information about Caecilius' various financial activities. Students often ask how Quintus could sell buried real estate! Ask the students what assets would have survived the eruption.

Stage Commentaries

This short passage links the Roman Britain section of Unit 2 (Stages 13–16) with the Alexandria section (Stages 17–20). In answer to the king's questions, Quintus begins to recount the story of his life after the death of his parents at Pompeii. Students should read the passage quickly, using the comprehension questions at the end as clues for meaning. After students have recited the answers to the questions and you have verified that these are correct, the class can perhaps translate the story together, each student contributing what he or she knows.

If time allows, ask further questions, e.g.:

Why is the king now so friendly to Quintus?
What was the name of Quintus' mother?
In Quintus' sentence *ego et ūnus servus superfuimus* (line 6), what is implied about the fate of Grumio and Melissa?
Who do you think was the freed slave? (Clues in the paragraph, e.g. *tam fidēlis*, and a recollection of Stage 12, should suggest Clemens.)
How had Clemens shown himself *tam fortis et tam fidēlis* (line 7)? (See Stage 12 "ad vīllam" and "fīnis.")
What direction did Quintus and his *lībertus* sail when they were going *ad Graeciam* (line 12)? And *ad Aegyptum* (line 16)?

There are two examples in this story of relative clauses introduced into the accusative + verb sentence pattern:

line 7 *servum, quī . . . fuerat, līberāvī.*
line 9 *omnēs vīllās, quās . . . possēderat, vēndidī.*

The lack of an expressed nominative may cause students difficulty; if so, write on the board some further examples of this pattern.

First Language Note (Pluperfect Tense)

This note is straightforward and is not likely to cause problems. Students should study the note and translate the examples. Younger students or those who do not understand the forms and uses of the pluperfect might go back to the model sentences and retranslate them. Or you might prefer to drill the formation of the forms, asking for the pluperfects of perfect forms, e.g. "If *dīmīsit* means 's/he sent away,' what would be the Latin for 's/he had sent away'?" Here and in similar drills, choose vocabulary from checklists past and present, conveniently grouped in Appendix A of this Manual, pp. 105–9 below.

Drills

Exercise 1   Type: completion
            Missing item: noun

Stage 16

Test of accuracy: sense and correct ending
Grammatical point being practiced: nominative and dative plural, introduced in Stages 5 and 9

If students complete this exercise as written homework, remind them, in advance, of the difference in spelling between "Britons" (the people) and "Britain" (the country).

Exercise 2 Type: translation
Grammatical point being practiced: imperfect and perfect tenses

The Durotriges were the tribespeople occupying the area around present-day Dorchester, in southwestern England. For discussion, ask students why Cogidubnus helped the Romans. The question whether Vespasian rewarded the king with an Italianate palace is controversial. If Fishbourne was a gift for services rendered, it may have been for help in keeping the legions in Britain loyal to Vespasian in his bid for the principate in A.D. 69.

This second exercise contains two examples of a new sentence pattern, dative + accusative + verb: *Rōmānīs frūmentum comparāvī. Rōmānīs explōrātōrēs dedī* (line 5). Students have previously met this pattern only in subordinate clauses (like *quod mihi auxilium . . . dedistī* in line 16 of this same exercise). If the pattern causes difficulty, write further examples on the board. An example of this pattern (*vigilibus rem nārrāvit*) is found in Diagnostic Test 4. The pattern recurs in the later stages of Unit 2 and is reviewed in the Unit 2 Review Grammar, p. 185, paragraph 6.

Second Language Note (Further Uses of the Infinitive)

After students have studied this note and translated the examples, repeat similar sentences from previous stories. In this stage, "rēx spectāculum dat" is the best quarry for infinitives.

The Background Material

The site of the palace is close to the sea; in Roman times it was even closer to the shoreline and there was a wharf only a few yards from the south wall of the palace. The earliest buildings on the site were military. They belong to the invasion period of A.D. 43 and may have been connected with Vespasian's attack on the Isle of Wight or his drive against the Durotriges to the west. By about A.D. 75, civilian buildings, constructed of timber and masonry, appear, among them a remarkable set of baths with at least seven heated rooms. The evidence suggests the presence by this date of a civil settlement of some size that had connections with Italy.

In A.D. 75 or thereabouts, work began on the palace itself. When

Stage Commentaries

finished, it consisted of four wings containing some sixty to seventy rooms, around a colonnaded courtyard. The total complex, which occupied an area of just over 5½ acres (2.25 hectares), has been described as "a piece of Italy planted in Britain." Two examples may be given of the expert skill lavished upon it:

1 The Builders' Working Area

Excavations uncovered a builders' working-area spread over six rooms. The whole area was blanketed in white sand from 1 inch to 1 foot (2.5 cm to 30 cm) thick, containing waste pieces of Purbeck marble, red and buff colored mudstone from the Mediterranean, gray shale from the Weald (in southeast England), and a small quantity of marble imported from central France and Italy. The work that went into the preparation of this decorative stone may be estimated from the calculation that in this working area there were 130 cubic feet (3.7 cubic meters) of waste stone. Examination of the waste suggests that the different operations involved—chipping, chiseling, grinding, and sawing—were each performed in a separate part of the area. At the point where the sawing appears to have been done, the largest deposits of sand were found. This amount of sand required some explanation, and archaeologists carried out an experiment. They discovered that a piece of marble could be cut effectively by means of a six-strand twisted copper wire in a hacksaw frame with the help of sand and water. The kind of cut made was exactly the same as that left by the Roman masons. This method of stone-cutting is still used in parts of Italy today.

The products of the workshop included patterned stone pieces of pavements, panels and moldings for wall veneers, small decorative pieces possibly for inlaying on furniture and various household utensils like mortars and pestles. Nearby were found traces of a service road used for bringing building materials to the site, and there were also some remains of timber buildings where the workmen may have lived. One can easily imagine the organization required to get such an operation going and to keep it up.

2 The Garden of the Great Court

Here again the work of experts is apparent. They removed over 7,000 cubic yards (5,350 cubic meters) of surface clay and gravel—an immense task even today with modern bulldozers—to expose the underlying clay bed. This was then resurfaced with topsoil. Shrubs and bushes were planted in a specially prepared mixture of loam and crushed chalk to counteract the acidity of the soil. Roses too were planted in specially dug flowerbeds. Archaeologists have exposed those beds and traced their

Stage 16

layout. The whole garden had (and has) a formal arrangement reminiscent of the garden of Pliny's villa in Tuscany. It leaves an unmistakable impression of Italy and Italian skill.

The question remains whether Cogidubnus lived here. Although there is no evidence, either of inscription or statue, to prove explicitly that he did, the most plausible explanation of this very unusual building is that it was a tangible sign of the emperor's great favor towards a loyal client-king. The most detailed description of the excavations will be found in Cunliffe *Excavations at Fishbourne* or, in a more readable account, in Cunliffe *Fishbourne*.

Suggestions for Further Work

1 Discuss the variety of craftsmen probably employed in the building and decoration of the palace at Fishbourne. What materials and tools did they use? Compare these with the materials, tools, and sources of power employed on a modern building. See Neuburger; it is out of print, but very helpful if one can locate a copy.
2 Ask younger students to write an imaginative account *either* of a visit by Cogidubnus to the palace while under construction (he may be showing it to a visiting chieftain, e.g. Dumnorix) *or* of masons at work cutting stone and marble in the mason's yard. Encourage students to research their topics and to be as detailed as possible about the skills and methods employed on the site. They might consult Neuburger, and Strong and Brown.
3 Discuss Roman taste as reflected in the layout, amenities, and decoration of their gardens. Base the discussion on information in the textbook about the palace garden, a picture of the garden of the villa of the Vettii at Pompeii (Filmstrip 1, frame 7), and other information in Jashemski. Compare Roman gardens with modern private ones and also with the elaborate gardens of stately homes and with city parks.
4 Show slides (filmstrip frames 10–12; slides 10–17) of the mosaics at Fishbourne. Discuss mosaics as luxury-furnishings, and compare them with later such furnishings as medieval tapestries and modern carpets, noting particularly the types of designs, human figures and/or geometrical patterns.

Stage Commentaries

STAGE 17: ALEXANDRĪA

BRIEF OUTLINE

Reading passages ⎫
Background material ⎭ the city of Alexandria

Chief grammatical points — genitive singular and plural
position of *enim, tamen,* and *igitur*

NARRATIVE POINTS			
A.D. Date	*Setting*	*Characters Introduced*	*Story Line*
Flashback (cont.): Winter 80	Alexandria: around the city	Barbillus (wealthy merchant), Diogenes (Greek friend of Barbillus), Plancus (a bore)	Quintus, visiting Barbillus in Alexandria, is given an Egyptian slave, who is killed when a crowd attacks Diogenes' house, where Quintus and the slave have taken refuge. Plancus bores Barbillus and Quintus in the marketplace. Barbillus tells story of Arab merchant carried off by monstrous bird, from whose nest he stole jewels now owned by Barbillus.

GRAMMATICAL POINTS

genitive singular and plural (in prepositional phrases)
 e.g. *prō templō Caesaris erat āra.*
position of *tamen, igitur, enim*
 e.g. *Serāpis enim est deus quī segetēs cūrat.*
obstō + dative
 e.g. *in triviīs magna multitūdō nōbīs obstābat.*
pluperfect (in main clause)
 e.g. *Barbillus hās gemmās ā mercātōre Arabī ēmerat.*
clauses with *sīcut*
 e.g. *hoc mōnstrum, sīcut pīca, rēs fulgentēs colligere solet.*
infinitive + *soleō, coepī, melius est*
 e.g. *nunc sacerdōtēs in ārā sacrificium facere solent.*

Stage 17

SENTENCE PATTERNS
DAT + V
   e.g. *puerō respondī.*
ACC + NOM + V
   e.g. *ita mercātōrem fortūna servāvit.*
V + NOM (increased incidence)
   e.g. *in hāc casā habitat faber. est Diogenēs, faber Graecus.*
increased complexity in subordinate clauses
   e.g. *in armāriō erant quīnque fūstēs, quōs Diogenēs extrāxit et nōbīs trādidit.*

Quīntus dē Alexandrīā

Quintus continues the account to Cogidubnus that he began in Stage 16, "Quīntus dē sē." Remind students of this. The model sentences introduce some of the most striking characteristics of Alexandria and feature the characters who are going to play leading parts in the next four stages. In particular, they describe Pharos, the huge and famous lighthouse which dominated the Great Harbor; also the Caesareum; and the sentences introduce Barbillus, the wealthy merchant who acts as host to Quintus and Clemens, and gives Quintus an Egyptian slave-boy.

The illustrations are filled with historical detail; students might want to discuss them before or after translating the captions underneath. Encourage such discussion by asking, say, why Quintus makes a sacrifice (p. 79), why he and Clemens are unshaven, or whose atrium Barbillus' more resembles, Cogidubnus' (Stage 16 model sentence, *tum ad ātrium vēnērunt*, p. 62) or Caecilius' (Stage 2, p. 19).

Each group of sentences contains an example of the genitive case, which is introduced in this stage. The context of each genitive should help students understand it. Thus in paragraph 1, several sentences with the accusative *portum* and nominative *Alexandrīa* anticipate the phrase *in portū Alexandrīae*.

tumultus

As the model sentences have shown, Quintus goes to live as a guest in the house of Barbillus, a former business acquaintance of Caecilius. With Barbillus' help, he has set Clemens up in the glass business which thrives near the harbor. Clemens is now a freedman, liberated by Quintus because of his bravery at Pompeii, and his experiences are described in the next stage. In the present stage, the scenes of Alexandrian life are observed through the eyes of Quintus.

Here Quintus describes his attempt to make his way through the city

Stage Commentaries

to visit Clemens, accompanied by his new slave-boy. They happen upon a volatile mob of Egyptians who are disaffected with the Greeks and Romans. Though the house of Barbillus' Greek friend Diogenes, which happens to be at hand, offers a temporary refuge, some Egyptians break into the house and the slave-boy is killed in the ensuing scuffle.

This story is about racial strife. It illustrates certain characteristics of such tensions; they are easily aroused, erupt quickly into violence, are directed at the nearest available target, and often involve the innocent. Students will notice that this theme is not entirely ancient, and they may show in their reactions to the story that they are aware of similar conflicts in today's society. Some classes may want to probe the causes—social, economic, and cultural—of tension between racial groups and the problems that governments have in easing or containing it. As for ancient Alexandria, why were the Egyptians envious and hostile toward the Greeks? Why were Jews in conflict from time to time with non-Jews? The issue of Jewish separatism could lead to the subject of the Jewish revolt in A.D. 66–70 and its tragic outcome at Masada in A.D. 73. The aftermath of this tragedy is recreated in Unit 3, Stage 29.

The multi-racial character of Alexandrian society often placed the governor in difficulties, since he could do little to relax the underlying tensions between the groups and generally had to rely on police methods to preserve public order. For centuries, the Greeks had held the highest positions of authority and influence; they formed a close-knit community and were skilled at retaining their advantages. Opposed to them were many other groups: Syrians, native Egyptians, and Jews, all struggling for a share of prosperity in what was predominantly a Greek city. Although students should not exaggerate the racial unrest in Alexandria, it was no doubt a chaotic city. Vigorous and competitive trade was its daily preoccupation; riot was perhaps its daily hazard. Students who are curious about racial attitudes in the ancient world might consult a translation of Juvenal *Satires* III and XV, or you might translate for them Martial's epigram, XI.96.

The sentence *nam in casā . . . vituperābant* (lines 31–32) may cause difficulty, since the point of the first half of the sentence only becomes clear when the second half has been read. If so, refer students to question 5 at the end of the story and to lines 20–21.

After the students have read and translated the story in class or as homework, encourage discussion with the questions in the textbook and others less specific, e.g.:

Why do you think the old man was making a speech (lines 20–21)?
What might he have said about the Greeks and Romans?
Why was Quintus worried (line 22)?

Why did Quintus (when he entered Diogenes' house) whisper rather than talk aloud (line 28)?

Why did Diogenes feel it necessary to keep a supply of clubs in his house?

Who do you think was to blame for the Egyptian boy's death?

ad templum

Barbillus and Quintus encounter Plancus, an educated, but insensitive bore who—like the similar character in Horace's *Satire* I.9—is impervious to polite discouragement. Plancus insists upon accompanying Quintus and Barbillus to the Temple of Serapis, and delivers a pedantic lecture on the worship of Serapis to his unwilling audience.

The god Serapis, worshipped together with Isis, was the guardian deity of Alexandria and was connected especially with the harvest and with healing. He became increasingly popular in the next century throughout the other provinces of the empire. At the Yorkshire Museum, in York, England, is a sandstone tablet (*C.I.L.* VII.240), describing the dedication of an otherwise unknown temple to Serapis—(expanded version):

Deo sancto Serapi templum, a solo fecit Cl(audius) Hieronymianus leg(atus) leg(ionis) VI vic(tricis).

Claudius Hieronymianus, general of the Sixth Legion Victrix, built [this] temple to the holy god Serapis from the ground up.

This inscription is decorated on either side with *caducei* (winged staffs with two serpents twisted around each staff), emblems of healing. Another inscription (*C.I.L.* VIII.2629), at Lambaesis, in Africa, from a base that once held the bust of a priest, describes this priest as:

Iovis Plutonis Serapis sacer(dos).
Priest of Jupiter Pluto Serapis.

Here the Egyptian Serapis is identified with the Greek Pluto, who was associated with grain-harvesting.

The religious activities surrounding the cult of Serapis and Isis are described more fully in Stage 19. In the meantime, notice that:

1 The large statue of the god was placed in the *cella*, or inner sanctuary, of the temple. Only priests and members of the brotherhood of Isis could enter this part of the temple; ordinary persons would have seen the statue only when it was brought out for a religious festival.
2 The performance of the public sacrifice took place outside the temple, not inside. (Contrast for students the position of an altar inside a modern Christian church.)

Stage Commentaries

3 The public were spectators rather than participants in the religious act. For more information, see Marlowe 59–61.

The photograph on p. 85 of Unit 2 shows Serapis crowned with a basket or grain-measure that indicates symbolically his connection with crops and fertility. The statue head, which had been sculpted in Italy, was found in the Romano-British ruins of a temple of Mithras (now reconstructed in front of Temple Court, Queen Victoria Street, in London, but popularly known, from its original location, as the Walbrook temple). The presence of Serapis' image in the temple of another deity, Mithras, well indicates the mutual tolerance of cults that was typical of the time.

Students might enjoy reading this story aloud expressively, either in chorus or with parts assigned. Rehearse with them particularly the lines of Barbillus, who can barely suppress his exasperation with the bore Plancus. Or students might enjoy listening (with their books open) to the vivid reading of this story on the first of the two audio-cassettes produced for the course.

Some Suggested Questions

Why was Barbillus reluctant to reply (line 10)?
Why did Plancus eventually *have* to keep quiet?
Would you have found Plancus a nuisance? If so, why?

First Language Note (Genitive Singular and Plural)

This note pulls together examples of the new, genitive forms which older, and sometimes younger, students translate easily. The list of further examples is a useful check on their understanding. If students need more practice, ask them to spot more examples of the genitive already met in the two previous stories. When translating, the students should provide as much variety as possible in translations. Thus *in portū Alexandrīae* may be translated "in the harbor of Alexandria" or "in the harbor at Alexandria"; *per viās urbis*, "through the city streets" or "through the streets of the city"; *in vīllā Barbillī*, "in the house of Barbillus" or "in Barbillus' house." Further examples of the genitive are provided for practice in the Unit 2 Review Grammar, p. 166.

mercātor Arabs

Quintus tells how, when having dinner with Barbillus on a certain occasion, Barbillus showed him an impressive collection of jewels. Barbillus described the adventures of the Arab merchant from whom he obtained the jewels. The merchant, transporting goods through the desert, was first attacked by bandits, and subsequently carried off by a monstrous bird which was attracted to the merchant's shiny belt. A captive in the bird's nest, the merchant discovered an enormous quantity of precious gems, which the bird had colleted. After gathering up as many of these as he could, the merchant climbed onto the bird's back while it slept, and when, next day, the bird flew over the sea, the merchant saw his opportunity, and plunged into the water near a ship which might rescue him.

Of the traders who converged on Alexandria from the east, some came by sea to the Red Sea ports and then via canal to the Nile river and down, while some came by overland routes through the desert (see map on p. 91 of Unit 2). Arab traders brought with them not only precious goods, but also marvelous tales of desert travel, the themes of which were grotesque incident, sudden wealth, and miraculous escape. Ask students at this point of the discussion, "With whom did the Alexandrians trade?" If students mention Arabia, tell them about the maritime silk and spice trade which Arab voyagers established with China and which gave rise to the folktales about Sindbad the Sailor. Some students might enjoy reading about the real-life recreation of Sindbad's voyage in a medieval Arab sailing vessel (planks tied together with rope made from the fiber of coconut shells) by Severin (see in Bibliography, p. 117). Severin's ship, called the Sohar after Sindbad's birthplace in Oman, sailed the 6000 miles between Muscat, in Oman, to Canton, in China, slowly but surely for seven months. Or some students might enjoy reading, in translation, the source of this passage, "The Second Voyage of Sindbad" in the *Arabian Nights*.

After students have translated the story, help fix it in their minds by asking questions, e.g.:

> How would you manage an ambush in the desert?
> What do you think the merchant expected the monster to do when it flew at him?
> Why in fact did the monster fly at the merchant?
> What caused the merchant's belt to shine?
> How would you have tried to escape from the nest?
> Would you have taken anything from the nest?
> Which parts of the story do you find hardest to believe?

Younger students might then want to discuss fabulous monsters, both aerial and maritime, like the Harpies of Greek myth or the Loch Ness monster or Bigfoot of the modern tabloid newspapers. You might contribute a description of the elk without leg joints which Caesar described in *De Bello Gallico* VI.27.

You might also ask a student with artistic ability to draw the bird-monster of this story on the blackboard or on an overhead projector acetate. Other students should search the textbook and suggest any additional details the artist may have forgotten.

Drill on grammar in this stage should include review of the relative clause and the pluperfect tense. Ask students to pick out examples of relative clauses and their antecedents in "tumultus" or "ad templum" (there are six examples in each story) and to identify the pluperfect tenses in "mercātor Arabs" (there are two). Always relate abstract terms like "relative clause" and "antecedent" to concrete examples.

The pluperfect tense, so far restricted to relative clauses, will appear from this point in main clauses as well. *mercātōrem fortūna servāvit* (p. 88, line 38) is the first example of a sentence with the pattern: accusative + nominative + verb. More examples will follow in Stages 18 and 19, together with the pattern: accusative + verb + nominative. There are also examples of these patterns in the Review Grammar, p. 185. Comment on the patterns is not necessary at this point.

Drills

Exercise 1   Type: completion
             Missing item: verb
             Test of accuracy: correct ending
             Grammatical point being practiced: 1st and 2nd persons singular and plural of imperfect and perfect tenses, introduced in Stage 12

Exercise 2   Type: completion
             Missing item: verb
             Test of accuracy: sense and correct ending
             Grammatical point being practiced: 1st, 2nd, and 3rd persons singular of present tense of *volō* and *possum*, introduced in Stage 13

Second Language Note (Position of enim, tamen and igitur)

This draws attention to the position of these connectives in the sentence and invites comparison with the position of their English equivalents. The position is admittedly a minor point, but it is one which students might easily overlook. If necessary with younger students, you might also write on the board one or two examples from the stories in this or previous stages.

The Background Material

This material is designed to help students think of Alexandria as a city which in size, culture, and economic importance was unique in the

Stage 17

eastern Mediterranean at this time. Students might usefully discuss the following points:

1 Its size, layout, and population. Perhaps a million people lived in an architect-designed conurbation spread over several square miles. It had been built up from nothing but a fishing village to be a showpiece of Alexander's empire. In the hands of his Greek successors, the Ptolemies, the city's natural advantages of large, safe anchorages on major trade routes were consolidated; the arts and scholarship flourished under royal patronage; Alexandria became a prosperous, international commercial center.
2 The style and method of its government. The administration was autocratic, with power concentrated in the hands of the Greek community. A highly developed bureaucracy controlled the life of the Egyptian peasants and villagers, whose work was prescribed to them in detail and whose freedom was severely restricted.
3 The city as a manufacturing center. For instance, it was famous for its papyrus.
4 The tensions which existed between the racial groups living in the city. For evidence of anti-semitism, see Lewis and Reinhold, II.413.
5 The contrasts between life in Alexandria, Pompeii, and Roman Britain. Levels of material comfort, cultural richness, personal freedom, and the general pace of life would have varied sharply between these places as well as between social groups. Ask students which of these places they would have preferred to live in and then invite them to debate their reasons.

Older students might want to compare with Alexandria certain large multi-ethnic American cities like New York and Los Angeles , where race riots have on occasion broken out, particularly in the hot summers, or, in Quebec, the city of Montreal, where certain French Canadians have sometimes agitated for separation from the supposedly English-dominated government of the Canadian confederation.
6 The city as the focal point of a very wide trade network. See the map in the students' textbook, p. 91. The purpose of this map is to show the extent of the empire at the time of the stories, and to indicate the main movements of goods both within and from outside the empire. Alexandria's importance as a trade center for both new materials and manufactured goods is clear. Silk came from China, pepper from India, and ivory from Central Africa. Rome imported far more than it exported; it paid for this with the revenue from its provinces.

The coin illustrated on p. 133 reflects the importance of shipping in the economic life of Alexandria and of Isis as the divine protector of the shipping trade.

Stage Commentaries

Words and Phrases Checklist

The genitive is now included in the checklists. Emphasize its meanings by asking the class for a translation not only of *hasta, latrō*, etc., but also of *hastae, latrōnis*, etc.

Suggestions for Further Work

The topic of Alexandria is well suited to group projects in which the research is shared out between groups and the results are combined to form a joint report. Visual material for Alexandria, however, is scanty. Little of the classical city remains to be seen, and this deficiency makes it difficult for many students to grasp its scale and significance (see above, pp. 6–11). The activities recommended below, therefore, concentrate on helping students enlarge their perception of life in a large city and so prepare them to grasp the magnitude and complexity of Rome itself, which they will meet in Unit 3.

Recreate for students much of the atmosphere of Alexandria by reading to them suitable extracts from Evans, unfortunately out of print, but still available in many libraries, or from Heuer or from Marlowe.

1 Help students picture the city. Begin by obtaining some data about any large modern city—its population, area, main industries, public facilities, university, local government, and the cultural and religious diversity of its population. Ask students to prepare a short "guide book" on the basis of this information. Then ask them to use such sources as Lewis and Reinhold, Marlowe, Forster's *Alexandria*, and the background material in Unit 2, Stages 17–20, to prepare a similar guide to Alexandria. Have students compare the two in class discussion.
2 Ask students to write a newspaper account, including an editorial, a feature article, and an eye-witness report, of a riot either between Jews and Greeks or between Greeks and Egyptians. Students should comment on the causes of the riot, the consequent damage, and the problem of law and order in the city. For the imaginary characters, students might use Greek names like Apollonius, Dionysius, and Hermaiscus; Jewish names like Philo, Josephus, Theophilus, and Markos; and Egyptian names like Phaseis, Zoilus, and Haryotis. As a variation on this activity, ask certain students to write "slanted" newspaper reports, dealing with the same incident, but written for newspapers with marked ethnic and editorial sympathies. Since in good newspapers such biases are rarely obvious, encourage students to be subtle in their portrayal of prejudice.
3 College and university students who have a good background in European literature, might want to write essays or reports on

Alexandria as an exotic literary locale. Recommended as primary sources, because they recreate modern life in a historical perspective, are the Greek poems of C.P. Cavafy (translated by Dalven or Keeley and Sherrard) or the "Alexandria Quartet" novels of Lawrence Durrell; the poet character Balthazar in these novels is a fictionalized representation of Cavafy. Recommended for their background information are Forster, *Pharos and Pharillon*; Keeley *Cavafy's Alexandria*; and Marlowe.

4 Ask students to consider Alexandria as a port. Ask them to list, after research, the major imports and exports, indicating where possible the origin of the goods; to draw a large plan of the Great Harbor; to sketch the Pharos lighthouse; to explore the evidence for the trade routes commonly used by land and sea, and for the kind of shipping and the length of some of the voyages made. See Lewis and Reinhold II.198–208; the McEvedy's *Penguin Atlas of Ancient History* 84–5; Hodge, Ch. V.

Or ask students to think about how a large modern port, e.g. New Orleans, New York City, or Vancouver, may differ from an inland city. Have them consider topics like the mixture of nationalities, influx of new ideas and customs, migrant populations, and the presence of trades and industries that relate primarily to ships and seafaring.

5 Because the Pharos lighthouse was one of the seven wonders of the ancient world, ask students to identify the other six and find as much about them as they can. "Which of the seven wonders still stands today?" (Answer: Great Pyramid of Cheops) Students will enjoy making their own choice of seven wonders in the *modern* world. Tabulate each individual's choices on the blackboard in order to determine whether there is any consensus among them.

6 Set a competition for the best story, in English, on the lines of "mercātor Arabs." The setting should be exotic or fantastic. Students might cast the story, for example, as the narrative of a silk trader talking to Barbillus, or a ship's captain talking to a wholesaler who has just purchased a consignment of Arabian perfume, or an elephant-hunter describing his adventures to a caravan merchant who has purchased a large amount of ivory. Read sections of the second and fifth voyages of "Sindbad the Sailor" before the students proceed to write their own story.

STAGE 18: EUTYCHUS ET CLĒMĒNS

BRIEF OUTLINE

Reading passages } economic and commercial life in Egypt
Background material } glassmaking

Chief grammatical points — agreement of adjective (gender)
verbs with dative (continued from Stage 11)

NARRATIVE POINTS

A.D. Date	Setting	Characters Introduced	Story Line
Flashback (cont.): Winter 80	Alexandria: glass stores of Clemens and Eutychus	Eutychus ("protection" racketeer)	Clemens, for whom Quintus has bought a glass store, is harassed by Eutychus and his gang for refusal to pay protection money. He is saved by cat, sacred to goddess Isis, whose devotee Clemens has become.

GRAMMATICAL POINTS

adjective: agreement of gender
    e.g. *tabernārius perterritus erat, quod senex vehementer clāmābat.*
    ancilla perterrita erat, quod multus sanguis fluēbat.
further examples of intransitive verbs: *cōnfīdō, appropinquō*, etc. + dative
    e.g. *nam tabernāriī, quī Eutychō pecūniam invītī dabant, paulātim Clēmentī cōnfīdēbant.*
genitive + nominative/accusative
    e.g. *Clēmēns officīnam Eutychī intrāvit.*
clauses with *ut* (= "as")
    e.g. *haec taberna, ut dīxī, prope templum deae Īsidis erat.*

SENTENCE PATTERNS
NOM/ACC + Q (genitive) + V
    e.g. *officīnam Eutychī intrāvit.*
increased incidence of DAT + ACC + V
    e.g. *ego Clēmentī diū tabernam quaerēbam.*
ACC + V + NOM
    e.g. *tabernam tuam dīripiunt Eutychus et operae.*
ACC + DAT + V
    e.g. *hanc tabernam Clēmentī emere volō.*
ACC + NOM + V
    e.g. *mox plūrimōs amīcōs Clēmēns habēbat.*
increased incidence of omission of verb in first of two clauses
    e.g. *Clēmēns vir fortis, nōn senex īnfirmus est.*
increased complexity of sentence structure:
(i) "branching" of one subordinate clause out of another
    e.g. *dīligenter labōrābant, quod aderat vīlicus, quī virgam vibrābat.*
(ii) "nesting" of one subordinate clause inside another
    e.g. *ubi ā templō, in quō cēnāverat, domum redībat, amīcum cōnspexit accurrentem.*

pugna

These groups of sentences describe the assault, referred to in the following story, on Barbillus' old freedman. After students have read them, they might discuss the characters in the pictures and the reasons for their actions. These sentences also illustrate gender agreement, but students need not discuss it until after the first language note, where it is set out in more detail. There is no new vocabulary.

taberna

This story explains how Clemens comes to own the store mentioned in Stage 17, "tumultus." He is established in business initially by Quintus who purchases some premises for him from Barbillus. The latter warns Quintus about the local protection racket, but the warning does not seem to carry any weight with the buyer, who reminds Barbillus that Clemens is quite capable of looking after himself.

During this and the following story, help students review noun forms by asking them to pick out examples of nouns in the nominative and accusative singular and plural. Ask questions, e.g. "What case is *servōs* in line 18 (of 'in officīnā Eutychī')?" and "Find a nominative in line 12 and say whether it is singular or plural."

Some Suggested Questions

What would be the advantage of putting all the glassware stores together in the same street? What would be the disadvantages?

Do you agree that Clemens was *fortis* (line 15)? If so, what had he done previously to show courage? (Students should remember that Clemens saved Iulius and sought out Caecilius during the climax of the Pompeii catastrophe, Unit 1, Stage 12.)

in officīnā Eutychī

Clemens, eager to take possession of his new store, is shocked to find that it has been ransacked. A neighboring storekeeper tells him to ask Eutychus who is responsible. Clemens locates Eutychus' workshop, forces his way past four huge guards, and confronts Eutychus, who greets him dismissively at first, and then, when he learns that Clemens is the owner of the ransacked store, addresses him with implied threats disguised as concern for Clemens' welfare. Clemens, however, proudly rejects Eutychus' offer of "protection," declaring that he can look after himself and his store.

This story brings out the characters of Clemens and Eutychus, and it provides insight into the running of a glass workshop. After reading and translating it, students might answer the questions below and also discuss the jobs being done by the various slaves and Eutychus' attitude toward them. If students ask in what ways the blown-glass vases were decorated (*ollās ōrnātās faciēbant*, lines 29–30), explain that a glassworker could have blown the glass "bubble" into a clay or wooden mold, imprinted it, and then removed it for further free blowing that would have expanded the design; he could have decorated the "bubble" while it was hot, raising knobs and ridges with pincers or indenting with same, or applying trails or blobs of different-colored liquified glass that were then "marvered," or pressed, into the surface; or he could have painted or engraved the vase after it was cooled. The glassmaking process is described on pp. 71–72 below. See also Price, "Glass," in Strong and Brown 111–25.

Students may translate *valvās ēvulsās vīdit, tabernam dīreptam* (lines 5–6) as "he saw the torn-off doors, the ransacked shop," but encourage better alternatives like "he saw the doors which had been torn off" and "he saw that the doors had been torn off and the shop looted." The phrase *officīnam Eutychī* (line 18) anticipates a pattern that appears frequently in Stage 19 and thereafter, nominative or accusative + genitive, but you need not comment at the moment.

Stage 18

Some Suggested Questions

Why does Clemens call the Egyptian guard in line 15 "Atlās?"
Why, in line 17, does Clemens refer to himself as *lībertō* rather than *mihi*?
Why does Eutychus show off his thirty slaves to Clemens?

Ask students to compare the price of the protection, ten gold pieces a year (line 38), with the price of the workshop, 100 gold pieces ("taberna," line 17). Discuss the morality of the racket by asking, e.g., "From what were the purchasers buying protection?"

Clēmēns tabernārius

Clemens soon prospers as a businessman, after repairing his damaged store. At this time, he also becomes a devotee of Isis, whose temple is located near his store, and he befriends a cat that lives in the temple by stroking her and giving food to her. Meanwhile, the other storekeepers in the neighborhood, who see Clemens doing well without paying off Eutychus, follow his example, and gradually stop paying the protection money themselves, whereupon Eutychus loses his temper and summons his thugs, announcing it is time to take action against Clemens.

The religious element of Alexandrian life, touched on in Stage 17 "ad templum," also reappears here, when Clemens joins the brotherhood of the goddess Isis and is initiated into the mysteries and the communal life of the cult. The members of the brotherhood meet regularly to celebrate the sacred meal, study the scriptures, and sing hymns and pray. Students will notice that these patterns of worship (discussed under Stage 19 in this Manual, pp. 82–84) are common to Judaism and Christianity. Explain that Middle-Eastern religions shared a common tradition in their liturgical and sacramental practices.

If students ask for more information about Isis, postpone a full discussion until Stage 19, where the subject is explored more fully. In the meantime, make the following comments: Isis was one of Egypt's most important goddesses, one of a closely related group of three deities—Isis, Osiris, and Horus. She was worshiped for her power to give new life in the form of crops in the spring or after the flooding of the Nile. She also offered hope of life after death to her followers.

After students have read and translated the story individually to themselves or by groups aloud, they might answer the questions in the textbook and others, like "Who does the phrase *ut dīxī* (line 7) imply was narrating the story?" or "Would Clemens not have made more profit if he had overcharged (cf. *pretium aequum semper postulābat*, line 6)?" While students are discussing the illustration on p. 104, ask whether Clemens looks *cōmis* or not. Students might also consider the reasons for the presence of a cat in the store, sitting by the counter. The ancient

Stage Commentaries

Egyptians kept cats both as pets and to keep down rats and mice in the many granaries of their fertile land. They also venerated cats as sacred animals, the earthly embodiments of their transcendent goddesses Isis and Bast.

First Language Note (Adjective Agreement: Gender)

This note concentrates on the gender agreement of noun and adjective. After students have studied the note, they should review the model sentences for this stage and, this time around, identify the adjectives and say with which nouns they agree.

Eventually, present examples where gender does not depend on sex or the noun and adjective are of different declensions, e.g. *cibus optimus* or *lībertus fortis*. Finally, write on the blackboard a mini-paradigm of adjectives in the nominative and accusative, masculine and feminine, singular and plural:

bonus   bona   bonī   bonae
bonum   bonam   bonōs   bonās,

and then ask students to use the appropriate form of these to translate adjectives in English sentences, e.g. "What is the Latin for 'good' in 'She loved her good son.'?" For additional practice sentences with adjectives, see the Review Grammar, p. 168.

Below are some nouns and adjectives from Stages 1–17 that might be used in drills like the ones suggested above; the words are selected from the checklists and the number in parentheses states the stage in which it appears in the checklist.

Nouns with gender which, in a Roman cultural context, is predictable:
   Masculine: *agricola* (5); *amīcus* (2); *centuriō* (7); *deus* (14); *dominus* (2); *fīlius* (1); *frāter* (10); *iūdex* (4); *marītus* (14); *nauta* (15); *pater* (1); *poēta* (4); *puer* (8); *rēx* (14); *sacerdōs* (15); *vir* (11).
   Feminine: *ancilla* (2); *domina* (14); *fēmina* (5); *māter* (1); *puella* (5).
   Neuter: *aedificium* (13); *cōnsilium* (16); *saxum* (15).

Nouns with gender which is, for us now, not suggested by the meaning:
   Masculine: *ānulus* (4); *cibus* (2); *cinis* (12); *clāmor* (5); *equus* (15); *faber* (5); *flōs* (16); *fundus* (12); *gladius* (8); *hortus* (1); *impetus* (17); *lectus* (15); *leō* (3); *liber* (10); *mōns* (12); *pēs* (8); *sanguis* (8).
   Feminine: *aqua* (15); *aula* (14); *cēna* (2); *cēra* (4); *coniūrātiō* (13); *epistula* (12); *fābula* (5); *flamma* (12); *fossa* (15); *gemma* (17); *gēns* (11); *hasta* (17); *iānua* (3); *īnsula* (17); *multitūdō* (17); *nūbēs* (12); *pāx* (10); *porta* (8); *sella* (14); *silva* (8); *taberna* (3); *turba* (5); *umbra* (7); *unda* (15); *urbs* (5); *via* (1); *vīlla* (3); *vīta* (17).
   Neuter: *agmen* (15); *dōnum* (14); *forum* (3); *imperium* (10); *lītus* (15); *mare* (17); *negōtium* (17); *tergum* (17).

Stage 18

Adjectives of the 1st and 2nd declensions:
  Adjectives which were originally perfect passive participles: *attonitus* (14); *contentus* (10); *exanimātus* (17); *parātus* (16); *perterritus* (4).
  Adjectives describing qualities: *benignus* (17); *bonus* (16); *callidus* (10); *ignāvus* (8); *sordidus* (17).
  Adjectives describing emotions: *fessus* (13); *laetus* (2); *sollicitus* (11).
  Antonyms: *magnus* (3)/*parvus* (6); *multī* (5)/*paucī* (17).
  Irregulars: *aeger, aegra, aegrum* (13); *pulcher, pulchra, pulchrum* (7).

Adjectives of the 3rd declension:
  Adjectives with one termination for m. & f., another for n.; ending with *-lis* or *-le*: *difficilis* (14); *facilis* (17); *fidēlis* (14); *līberālis* (11); *mīrābilis* (12); *nōbilis* (14); *ūtilis* (11).
  Adjectives with one termination for m. & f., another for n.; ending with *-is* or *-e*: *familiāris* (14); *fortis* (6); *omnis* (7).
  Adjectives with single termination for m., f., & n.: *ferōx* (8); *ingēns* (7); *mendāx* (4).

prō tabernā Clēmentis

Clemens hears the news that his store has been ransacked by Eutychus and his thugs. Far from being afraid, Clemens shows the faith of an Isiac, an initiate into the cult of the Egyptian goddess Isis, and standing up to the criminals, he is duly rewarded by the intervention of the sacred cat. Allow students to read and translate this story as rapidly as possible, since they will be eager to find out what is going to happen next. The story is also well suited to various kinds of dramatic presentation.

ubi ā templō, in quō cēnāverat, domum redībat, amīcum cōnspexit accurrentem (lines 2–3) is a new sentence pattern containing two subordinate clauses, one of which (*in quō cēnāverat*) "nests" within the other (*ubi ā templō . . . domum redībat*). The student's task is to handle the interruption of one statement while he or she accommodates another and to recognize the clause boundaries. To help with this, the editors have placed commas, for the time being, to mark the boundaries.

If students translate *tabernam tuam dīripiunt Eutychus et operae* (lines 4–5) as a passive construction, "your workshop is being ransacked by Eutychus and his thugs," do not dismiss it as totally wrong, but encourage students to begin with Eutychus and rephrase their translation.

Ask students to pick out examples of the dative case from the stories in this stage in order to prepare them for the second language note on pp. 111–12 of Unit 2. Review the sentences which contain clauses with *postquam, quod, simulac,* etc. in the Review Grammars of Unit 1 (p. 212) and Unit 2 (pp. 186–88).

Some Suggested Questions

Why do you think Clemens was not impressed by Eutychus and his thugs? Was it because his piety or religious faith protected him from fear? Or had he learned to stand up for himself during his former life as a slave? How did Clemens behave before he became a freedman? What do you think of the thugs' reaction to the cat? Credible? Incredible? (Students' views often differ surprisingly on this point.)

Drills and Further Practice

Exercise 1 Type: completion
　　　　　　Missing item: noun + adjective phrase
　　　　　　Test of accuracy: correct ending
　　　　　　Grammatical point being practiced: nominative singular and plural, introduced in Stages 1 and 5

Exercise 2 Type: completion
　　　　　　Missing item: verb
　　　　　　Test of accuracy: correct ending
　　　　　　Grammatical point being practiced: 3rd person singular and plural of pluperfect tense, introduced in Stage 16
　　　　　　Grammatical point incidentally practiced: relative clause

Students are likely to treat *dīrepta* in sentence 2 as an adjective (as in the stories) and translate "was ransacked." An occasional student may ask, "Would it not be clearer to say 'had been ransacked'?" You should agree, but not anticipate the Unit 3 discussion of the indicative passive with a premature analysis.

Exercise 3 Type: completion
　　　　　　Missing item: verb
　　　　　　Test of accuracy: sense and correct ending
　　　　　　Grammatical point being practiced: 1st and 2nd persons singular of perfect tense, introduced in Stage 12

Different types of perfect formation are included in this exercise: the perfect stem in *-s-*, the strong perfect stem, and the perfect stem in *-v-*. Observe whether some formations cause more difficulty than others and, if necessary, make up further examples, keeping the vocabulary simple or familiar and the sentences short. Use nouns from the list above on p. 68, and perfects from the list below; all the verbs are selected from the checklists in Stages 1–17 and the number in parentheses states the stage in which a given verb appears in the checklist.

　　Perfects with *-v-*: *agitāvit* (8); *ambulāvit* (5); *appropinquāvit* (17); *audīvit* (5); *cantāvit* (13); *clāmāvit* (3); *complēvit* (12); *cupīvit* (9); *petīvit* (5); *pūnīvit* (15); *quaesīvit* (4); *saltāvit* (16).

Perfects with -u-: *dēsiluit* (17); *exercuit* (9); *habuit* (4); *iacuit* (12); *placuit* (11); *posuit* (16); *potuit* (13); *rapuit* (11); *retinuit* (13); *tacuit* (10); *tenuit* (15); *timuit* (12).

Perfects with -s- or -x- (=-cs-): *āmīsit* (12); *clausit* (15); *cōnsēnsit* (16); *cōnspexit* (7); *cōnsūmpsit* (8); *dērīsit* (16); *dīxit* (13); *fulsit* (17); *haesit* (17); *hausit* (13); *īnspexit* (9); *intellēxit* (7); *plausit* (5); *scrīpsit* (6); *prōcessit* (7); *surrēxit* (3); *trāxit* (13).

Strong perfects: *advēnit* (13); *cēpit* (10); *effūgit* (16); *ēgit* (4); *ēmit* (6); *lāvit* (14); *lēgit* (11); *recēpit* (17); *sēdit* (1); *vīcit* (15); *vīdit* (3).

Perfects with stem unchanged: *bibit* (3); *contendit* (5); *dēcidit* (13); *incidit* (12); *ostendit* (9); *respondit* (3); *ruit* (13); *vertit* (16).

Perfects with reduplicated consonant: *crēdidit* (11); *cucurrit* (5); *dedit* (9); *stetit* (5); *trādidit* (9); *vēndidit* (4).

Perfects from stem different from the present one: *fuit*, present *est* (1); *obtulit*, present *offert* (9); *sustulit*, present *tollit* (16); *tulit*, present *fert* (9).

Second Language Note (obstō, resistō, etc. with Dative)

This note draws attention to verbs which take the dative, a number of which students have now met. When they have studied the note, write examples from previous stories on the board or make up your own sentences. Below are some verbs, selected from the checklists in Stages 1–17, which take the dative; the number in parentheses states the stage in which the verb appears in the checklist.

Verbs taking the dative: *appropinquāre* (17); *crēdere* (11); *favēre* (11); *placēre* (11); *praeesse* (15); *prōmittere* (11); *respondēre* (3); *superesse* (16).

The Background Material

The topic of Alexandria is continued. We turn now from racial tension in the city to commercial activity, both reputable and otherwise. The worship of Isis is also mentioned, but postpone discussion until Stage 19, where it becomes the main feature.

From about 3000 B.C. in the Middle East, glass because of its special qualities was increasingly used to make both practical and ornamental objects. The popularity of glass resulted from its versatility: it could be colorless or colored, transparent, translucent, or opaque; it weighed, when compared to fired clay or metals, very little; it could be easily cleaned, as it was impermeable to liquids, and reused (contrast the rough interior of terracotta pots); although fragile, it could last a long time; and finally it could be made into graceful, beautifully decorated shapes. Among the special qualities of glass was its viscosity, which allowed it, when heated, to turn from a cold, hard solid into a hot, syrup-like liquid. As the heat in the crucible was increased and the glass became more malleable, the glass could be removed and shaped by various techniques which accumulated with the centuries. And when the glass was quickly cooled, its shape was fixed.

The oldest techniques for manipulating semi-liquid glass were the trailing of glass-syrup around rod-centered cores made of friable, removable materials and the forcing of glass-syrup into or around terracotta or metal molds. These ancient, laborious, time-consuming techniques were suitable only for shaping small objects like perfume bottles, tableware, beads, jewelry, inlays, and plaques. Larger objects would have necessitated extremely long rods and gigantic molds. The tombs of the nobility of Pharaonic, pre-Greco-Roman Egypt have provided museums with the most beautiful examples of the kinds of ancient glass listed above. See e.g. Grose, Figure 1, in Kingery and Lense.

The techniques of free blowing and blowing into molds developed three millenia later, in Roman times, and are still being used today (see the photograph, in the students' textbook, p. 113, of a contemporary worker at the Corning, NY, Glass Center, free-blowing a large glass jar). By the fourth century B.C., Syro-Palestine had become the major center, in the Mediterranean world, of glass manufacture, probably because wood for the charcoal, which was necessary for firing at the extremely high temperatures demanded in glass-kilns, was more readily available from the mountain-forests of Lebanon than it had been in the arid terrain of Egypt. It was somewhere in the Syro-Palestinian area that glassworkers developed the technique of blowing into semi-liquid-glass gobs (attached to the end of iron tubes) and forcing the gobs to bulge and then expand, like bubbles, into hollow glass balls. (There is a photograph of pieces from a glass blower's tube of the Roman period in Strong and Brown 117.) These balls could be reshaped or cut as they cooled, or—as it was soon discovered—they could be blown directly into hinged molds and shaped simultaneously as they were blown.

By blowing molten glass, rather than trailing or wrapping it around molds or casting it inside molds, glassworkers facilitated the production of innumerable additional shapes and, of course, larger sizes. In the first century A.D., this new technology led to an expansion of the glass industry all over the Roman empire, especially in those areas like Gaul, Germany, and Britain where the wood for fueling kilns was plentiful. The old core and casting techniques were gradually discontinued, and the simplicity of the new blowing technique facilitated the production of vast quantities of cheap glasswares which could be afforded by all classes of Roman society. By A.D. 80, the year Quintus set Clemens up in business, glass products were being imported into Alexandria in large quantities and widely sold to eager urban purchasers.

Stage 18

In addition to the glass-import business, there may also have been a small glassmaking industry in Alexandria. The tradition of glassmaking in Egypt was very old, much older in fact than Alexandria itself. There is little archaeological evidence, however, for a major glass-manufacturing industry in Alexandria.

For further information about the history of glass technology, see Harden; the section by J. Price in Strong and Brown 111–25; the sections by D. Grose in Klein and Lloyd 9–38 and in Kingery and Lense 65–79. For further information about the economic life of Roman Alexandria, see Lewis and Reinhold II.198–208, 363–64, 397–400; Fraser I.131–88; Lewis *Life* 134–55.

Words and Phrases Checklist

From now on, 1st and 2nd declension adjectives are shown in these lists in the form of the masculine, feminine and neuter nominative singular; 3rd declension adjectives are usually shown in their masculine form only. To be sure that students are clear about this, ask them, e.g., "What would be the Latin word for 'sacred' if it described a woman?" or "What is the neuter form of the word for 'long'?" With a few examples of this kind, students should be able to grasp the new layout.

Suggestions for Further Work

1 If you own or can borrow a copy of Lindsay *Daily Life in Roman Egypt* (now out of print), provide students with a selection of data from pp. 258ff. and ask them to build up from it a written account of life on the estate of Lucius Bellenus Gemellus at the time of our story. Epagathus is the supervisor.
2 Read with the class extracts from the *Acts of the Apostles*, e.g. 19.23–41; 21.27–40; 22.1–30, and then discuss them as instances of civil disturbance in the Roman provinces.
3 Read with the class the account of St. Paul's stormy voyage from Caesarea to Rome (*Acts of the Apostles* 27 & 28.1–16) and ask students, using this as a basis, to compose an imaginary account by an ordinary sailor of a voyage in a grain ship from Alexandria to Rome. The story will be more lively if it is written in the first person. Encourage students to describe personalities as well as natural disaster.
4 Students will enjoy visiting a demonstration of glass blowing. The technique has changed very little from the time it was first invented. There are frequently demonstrations in many historical parks, like those at Williamsburg, VA; at Sturbridge, MA; the Black Creek Pioneer Village, in North York, Ontario; and especially the Corning, NY, Glass Center, where there is a fascinating model of a

turn-of-the-century glass factory with miniature workers holding tiny facsimiles of many tools unchanged since Roman times.

North American museums with excellent collections of Roman glass are the Los Angeles County, CA, Museum; the Metropolitan Museum of Art, New York City; the Royal Ontario Museum, Ontario; and especially the Corning, NY, Museum of Glass.

5 Younger students could paint Roman or Egyptian designs on cheap glassware (see slides 32–39). (Additional slides are available for purchase from The Corning Museum of Glass, One Museum Way, Corning, NY 14830–2253; telephone 607-937-5371.) Particularly they might enjoy painting Isis in an Egyptian setting of, say, obelisks and pyramids, Isis and her dog Anubis, or her sacred, Siamese-like cat. Many of the illustrations or photographs in Stages 17–20 would provide suitable inspiration. Or students might prefer to draw and color with felt-tip pens on paper some of the Roman glassware which is illustrated in the textbook (pp. 100, 101 and 103) or in the plates of Strong and Brown.

STAGE 19: ĪSIS

BRIEF OUTLINE

Reading passages } Isis worship
Background material }

Chief grammatical points *hic*
imperative (including *nōlī*, *nōlīte*)
vocative

Stage 19

NARRATIVE POINTS

A.D. Date	Setting	Characters Introduced	Story Line
Flashback (cont.): March 5, 81	Alexandria: city and harbor	Aristo (Greek amateur tragedian), Galatea (his wife), Helena (their daughter)	Family quarrels between Aristo, Galatea, and Helena provide a comic interlude to sacred procession of goddess Isis.
Flashback (cont.): Spring 81	Barbillus' estate on the Nile river	Phormio (Barbillus' estate-manager), Barbillus' personal astrologer	Barbillus' astrologer warns him against hunting; Barbillus goes hunting anyway, but is attacked by a hippopotamus, his boat capsizes among the crocodiles, and he is wounded by a slave's spear in the mêlée.

GRAMMATICAL POINTS
increased incidence of *hic*
  e.g. *haec fēmina est Galatēa.*
increased incidence of *nōlī, nōlīte*
  e.g. *iuvenēs! cēdite! nōlīte nōbīs obstāre!*
increased incidence of genitive + nominative/accusative
  e.g. *puellae corōnās rosārum gerunt.*
genitive of adjective
  e.g. *quam raucae sunt vōcēs fēminārum Graecārum!*
fīō + predicative nominative
  e.g. *aqua līmōsior fīēbat, harundinēsque dēnsiōrēs.*

No new SENTENCE PATTERNS in this stage.

Model Sentences

The model sentences introduce a Greek family: Aristo, his wife Galatea, and his daughter Helena. They watch the spring procession at Alexandria in honor of the goddess Isis. Students will be able to understand and discuss the procession better if they read the relevant parts of the background material first.

The genitive case, of which use so far has been restricted to prepositional phrases (with the single exception of *officīnam Eutychī*

Stage Commentaries

intrāvit, Stage 18, p. 102, lines 18–19), is now introduced in phrases where it depends on a nominative or accusative. The context gives strong clues to the meaning. This new development is not discussed in the language notes because students generally grasp it through experience.

The model sentences also contain several examples of the forms of *hic*, which is discussed in the first language note.

The following word and phrase are new: *castīgat, corōnās rosārum*.

Aristō

This easy passage, which extends the model sentences, exhibits the new genitive phrases in a clearly structured setting. A Greek family appears which comprises Aristo, a rather timid man and an unsuccessful writer of tragedies; Galatea, his wife, who is inclined to be assertive; and their daughter Helena, who is very interested in young men (and they in her!). Neither mother nor daughter shares Aristo's taste in literature; theirs is the popular culture of light music, novels, and verse which existed in the Hellenistic world side by side with more serious art.

diēs fēstus

In this story, Quintus tells of attending the festival of Isis in the company of Aristo, Galatea, and Helena, Barbillus having other things to do that day. On the way to the harbor, Galatea nags Helena and Aristo incessantly. When it turns out that the family's usual spot for viewing the annual procession has been occupied by two young men (Aristo evidently having forgotten to send a slave ahead to reserve the place), Galatea imperiously insists on their yielding their position, which they do with reluctance. Then the festivities begin.

The religious theme of this and the next two stories is discussed in the notes on the background material, pp. 82–84 below. While reading these stories with the class, try to bring out the sense of holiday, excitement, and spectacle, chiefly by encouraging students to visualize the scene.

The Alexandrians are thoroughly enjoying themselves and are no doubt dressed suitably for the occasion. The character of the speakers emerges through what they say. For instance, Galatea's pleasure in taking charge can be heard in

> "*Helena! nōlī festīnāre! tolle caput!*" (line 14).
> "*Aristō! nōnne servum māne ēmīsistī?*" (lines 21–22).
> "*iuvenēs! cēdite! nōlīte nōbīs obstāre!*" (line 35).

Whereas Aristo's instinct for a quiet life is obvious enough in

> "*cārissima, melius est nōbīs locum novum quaerere.*" (lines 29–30).

Stage 19

After students have read and translated the story, they should answer the comprehension questions at the end. In addition, you might ask them to reread the first paragraph and tell the reasons for the Isis festival. During discussion, students might compare this with modern spring festivals like Easter, May Day, Purim, or the Hindu festival of Holi.

If a student translates *viās urbis iam complēbant cīvēs Alexandrīnī* (lines 11–12) as "The streets of the city were now being filled by Alexandrian citizens," guide, without discouraging, him or her to a more literal rephrasing.

Begin review of grammar by using the Unit 2 Review Grammar. See pp. 95–97 below for guidance.

pompa

The procession passes by and its various features are admired by the spectators; Helena comments on the flowers being scattered in the path of the parade. The displaced young men, however, cannot see the parade, although they remark on Helena's beauty; this alarms Galatea, who renews her scolding of Aristo. Eventually, one of the young men accidentally steps on Galatea's foot in his efforts to see the procession. She gives him a tongue-lashing, and when Helena tries to defend him, Galatea turns on her as well. Aristo manages to settle her down, but laments to Quintus that writing tragedies comes naturally to him, because his "whole life is a tragedy."

Students will enjoy this story in several ways. They may take it simply as an amusing incident in the crowd, or as a further exploration of the contrasting characters of Galatea and Aristo, or as a study of psychology, illustrating the point that people tend to notice what interests them. Helena's eye is caught by the flowers; the young men's by Helena; and Galatea's by the yellow dress of the statue. After students, singly, in groups, or as a class, have translated the story in a straightforward manner, they should listen to it again, read aloud on the audio-cassette or by you, and then focus on the different elements by answering questions, e.g.:

> How would you describe Galatea's behavior toward the two young men? Is she fair to Aristo? Give reasons for your answer.
> Does Helena seem as quick to criticize as her mother? (Students should note *hic iuvenis tibi forte nocuit,* line 32.)
> Why, somewhat unexpectedly, does Galatea criticize her husband (*Aristō! cūr mē nōn servās? uxōrem fīliamque floccī nōn facis,* line 36)?
> Do the young men mind not having a good view of the procession? Why can they not see it?
> Is this story more about some of the spectators than it is about the procession? Explain your answer.

Stage Commentaries

During subsequent discussion, ask if any class members have seen a procession or pageant and if any particular details caught their attention in the way that the details of the procession of Isis attracted the notice of Galatea and Helena. Should students not understand how the four priests carried the statue *in umerīs* "on their shoulders" (line 23), ask them to look again at the picture on the title page.

If students ask questions about the textbook picture on p. 135, explain that from left to right, the priests and priestesses are carrying a sistrum, or rattle, a ladle, a pitcher of sacred water, a scroll, and a water-vessel. The falcon and lotus headdresses and the cobra are all Egyptian religious emblems.

The position of *inquit* in the sentence now becomes more idiomatic, e.g. *Helena "māter" inquit*. If necessary, help the students with this at first.

nāvis sacra

The sacred boat, heavily adorned with flowers, is launched, preceded by prayers to Isis, and followed by applause from the spectators, who then disperse to rejoice, while the priests carry the effigy of Isis back to her temple. On the walk home, Galatea, who has resumed nagging Aristo, does not at first notice that Helena is walking with the two young men. When Aristo calls her attention to what is going on, she at once concludes that the young men are bothering Helena, but Aristo observes that, if anything, the reverse appears to be true.

If students have not yet read the background material at the back of the stage, they should do so before attempting this story. Explain that the ship herself was only a ceremonial vessel. She carried no crew, but when filled with flowers and released from her moorings, simply drifted out to sea, never—one assumes—to be seen again. Alternatively, Griffiths 46–47 suggests that the ship was manned and sent to a destination like the sacred island of Delos.

Galatea continues to worry about her daughter meeting the young men, either not understanding or perhaps deliberately ignoring the fact that the men's interest is, under the circumstances, quite natural. Certainly, she seems not to notice, as does her husband Aristo, that Helena is encouraging the young men and, toward the end of the story, even keeping them company. Remind students that in antiquity, because well-born daughters were quite protected from suitors, they had little opportunity to meet young men except at public ceremonies and festivals. Slave-women, ironically, sometimes had greater freedom; students might recall the relationships of Melissa or Poppaea with Grumio in Unit 1.

Stage 19

Some Suggested Questions

Do you think that the Alexandrians wasted money when they outfitted a ship that was allowed to drift away?
Why do you think that Galatea imagined that the young men were "bothering" her daughter Helena?
Who has better powers of observation, Aristo or Galatea?

In the few minutes remaining at the end of the period, review the forms of 3rd declension nouns, several of which appear in this story: *sacerdōs, sacerdōtis*, m.; *spectātor, spectātōris*, m.; and a string of nouns whose genitive form is the same as the nominative: *puppis*, f.; *nāvis*, f.; *cīvis*, m.f.; *auris*, f.; *iuvenis*, m. Write paradigms on the board, but let students suggest the appropriate forms; then ask students what would be the Latin of the nouns in English sentences, e.g. "The stern *of the ship* was filled with flowers" or "The young men had large *ears*." (Answers: *nāvis, aurēs*.) Because the gender of 3rd declension nouns is so frequently unpredictable, you might also go on, after the students have been drilled on forms, to write the nominatives on the board along with their gender abbreviation and then ask volunteers to translate the *adjectives* in English sentences containing the nouns, e.g. "The young men had *large* ears" or "The *small* stern was decorated." (Answers: *magnās, parva*.) The advantage of such a drill is that it helps students fix the gender of Latin nouns in their mind. To prepare for this drill, consult the selection of adjectives (from the checklists) above on p. 69 of this manual and, if students have forgotten them, write some on the board.

First Language Note (hic)

This note brings together the forms of *hic* which students have already met. When students have studied the note and translated the examples, make up English sentences with "this" or "these" in them and ask that volunteers translate the pronoun with the appropriate form from the paradigm provided in the note, e.g. "Galatea saw *these* young men." (Answer: *hōs*) If students have not already begun a grammar notebook, they might want to begin one now and write the paradigm for *hic* in the part of the notebook reserved for pronouns. Younger students should leave space for the neuter plural forms; older students might prefer to learn from you what these are and write them in ahead of time.

vēnātiō

Barbillus invites Quintus and Aristo to go crocodile hunting with him at his estate on the Nile. Barbillus' astrologer tries to stop the expedition, saying it is unlucky for Barbillus to go out on this particular day, but

Stage Commentaries

when Quintus derides the astrologer, Barbillus decides to ignore the warning, and go hunting anyway. At the estate, Phormio, Barbillus' manager, has prepared everything, and the hunt begins. All is going well, with many crocodiles taken, until a hippopotamus upsets Barbillus' boat. In the ensuing confusion, Barbillus is rescued, but not before he has been seriously wounded by the spear of one of his own slaves.

In this story, action and danger are the order of the day. Students should translate right to the end with minimal interruption from you. Events prepare the way for the death of Barbillus in Stage 20. Help students visualize the setting for the hunt by discussing the photograph on pp. 128–29 of Unit 2; it shows a detail from the famous Nilotic mosaic found at Praeneste, Italy. An interesting account of a hunt on the Nile will be found in Evans 190–95, and information on hunting generally in Lindsay *Leisure and Pleasure in Roman Egypt*, pp. 192–213.

Make certain, at the beginning, that the class understands the initial sequence of events, since everything happens rather quickly. Barbillus has invited Quintus and Aristo to a hunt. On the day itself, he first sends out Phormio with slaves and two small goats (which will be killed for bait). Then the hunting party, consisting of Barbillus, Quintus, and Aristo, emerges from the house in order to set out. At that moment, the astrologer rushes up to persuade them not to go.

Stress the atmosphere of foreboding which the words of the astrologer create. Students might want to discuss modern equivalents of the Chaldaean amulet, e.g. St. Christopher medals, mezuzahs, rabbit paws, or miniature horns. The reference to the Chaldaei in line 13 points to the main source of astrology in the Hellenistic and Roman world. The Chaldaei, named after the Chaldaeans whose capital city was Babylon, were an ancient priesthood; they had developed both the early scientific study of astronomy and the pseudo-science of astrology. For more information about the Chaldaei, see *Cambridge Ancient History* XI.642–43.

Some Suggested Questions

Is the astrologer's reason for anxiety convincing? What examples of this kind of belief about the stars can you suggest from modern life?
Was Barbillus on good terms with his slaves? Give evidence from the passage to support your answer (e.g. *omnēs rēs tibi parāvimus*, line 19).
Would you have enjoyed a hunt of this kind?

Second Language Note (Imperative Singular and Plural, including nōlī, nōlīte)

This note sets out examples of the imperative, both singular and plural, as well as a note on *nōlī* + infinitive. If some students are puzzled by the

Stage 19

infinitive, ask them, "Does the literal meaning of *nōlī*, 'be unwilling!' explain the form of *currere?*" Students usually find imperatives easy to learn. Younger students enjoy responding physically to commands from the teacher, like the following derived from some verbs in the checklists: *sedē!* (1) / *surge!* (3); *hūc advenī!* (13) / *hinc fuge!* (12); *scrībe mihi* (6) *epistulam!*; you might begin with *cāre discipule* or *cāra discipula—fer mihi* (9) *illum librum* (or *illam rem*)!; *pulsā* (6) *hanc iānuam!*; *exī!* (3) / *intrā!* (2). The class enjoys performing the following commands as a unit: *tollite* (16) *dextram manum* (or *sinistram manum*)! followed immediately by *nōlīte tollere dextram manum!*; *spectāte* (5) *ad dextram* (or *ad sinistram*)!; *vertite* (16) *caput!* followed immediately by *nōlīte vertere caput!*; *surgite!* (3) followed immediately by *sedēte!* (1).

Drills

Exercise 1   Type: completion
  Missing item: verb
  Test of accuracy: correct ending
  Grammatical point being practiced: 3rd person singular and plural of perfect tense, introduced in Stages 6 and 7
  Set the above drill as a written quiz. If students have difficulty, review with them the sections on "Verbs" and "Irregular Verbs" in the Unit 2 Review Grammar, pp. 178–84.

Exercise 2   Type: completion
  Missing item: clause
  Test of accuracy: sense, based on story "diēs fēstus"
  Grammatical point being practiced: subordinate clauses with the indicative (*postquam, quod, simulac,* and *quamquam*)
If students find this exercise difficult, you might let them determine the answers by working in groups.

Exercise 3   Type: completion
  Missing item: case endings of nouns
  Test of accuracy: correct endings
  Grammatical point being practiced: nominative, accusative, dative, and genitive singular and plural, introduced in Stages 1, 2, 5, 8, 9, and 17
This exercise is designed to review all the above cases and to indicate whether you should drill any of them further. If necessary, students might study the section on "Nouns" in the Unit 2 Review Grammar, pp. 162–66.

Stage Commentaries

Third Language Note (Vocative Singular and Plural)

This note illustrates the slight differences in vocative endings. Invite students to look at the examples in paragraph 2. Ask them what *fīlius*, *Salvius*, *Holcōnius* have in common that *servus*, *amīcus*, *Eutychus* do not. Of course students do not need to know the rules about vocatives in order to translate from Latin into English, but they may be reassured to see that there *is* a rule and that variation of the vocative in Latin is not just random or capricious.

The Background Material

In the Greco-Roman world of the first century A.D., mystery religions exercised a pervasive influence. The cult of Isis, described in Stages 18 and 19, was one of these religions, and it is particularly interesting for two reasons. In the first place, it was the religion that Alexandria passed on to the ancient world. When the Ptolemaic rulers imposed on the city a new official state cult, that of Serapis, they incorporated into it the old Egyptian myth of Osiris-Isis which they gradually tried to purge of its former gruesome elements. The official cult image of Serapis, fashioned by the Greek sculptor Bryaxis and housed in the Serapeum designed by Parmeniscus, gave this old Egyptian god a Greek form (as in the photograph of Serapis in Unit 2, p. 85; filmstrip or slide 28). Nevertheless, it was the more primitive, life-giving Isis (see photograph on p. 125) who exerted a stronger hold on people's affections; it was Isis rather than Serapis whose worship spread from Alexandria throughout the Mediterranean. Established in Rome by the first century B.C., she was banished from time to time from the city center, where only the official Roman deities could properly be honored. In time, however, the cult received official recognition from the Emperor Gaius Caligula and was held in high regard by the Flavian emperors. For further information on the Mediterranean cult of Isis, see Solmsen, Ch. 2.

In the second place, it is interesting to observe resemblances between the worship of Isis and Christianity. These are discernible in the cult's religious concepts—e.g. sin, atonement, resurrection, trinity in the godhead—and also in its modes of worship that included the sacraments of baptism and communion, the use of incense, flowers, lights, music, choirs, adoration of relics, and the veiling of heads by women. Such parallels were not entirely or even largely coincidental. Although some of these elements clearly derive through Judaism from a substratum of common Near-Eastern religious phenomena, others also show the tendency of the early Christian church to assimilate, from contemporaneous religions, various ideas and practices that could be harmonized with its own orthodoxy.

Stage 19

The ancient resurrection myth of the Osiris-Isis cult functioned, among other things, as an allegory of nature. The drowning of Osiris, brother and husband of Isis, symbolized the flooding of the Nile. When the villain god Seth scattered pieces of Osiris' dismembered body throughout Egypt, he was symbolically planting crops. When Isis and her goddess sister Nephthys resurrected Osiris, they restored, not his life, but his sexual potency; thus Isis conceived and gave birth to Osiris' son Horus, himself a symbolic growing crop of grain. In the symbolic pageantry of the Egyptian dynasts called Pharaohs, the name Osiris was assigned to the Pharaoh when he died; the name Horus, to his son and successor; the name Isis, to the queen mother. Osiris, Isis, and Horus, therefore, formed a family trinity.

A vivid impression of Isis is given by Apuleius in the *Metamorphoses* (also known as the *Golden Ass*) XI.3–4, where she appears in answer to the fervent prayers of Lucius:

> Her long hair fell softly in ringlets on her divine neck, and was crowned with an intricate wreath in which were entwined all kinds of flowers. Just above her forehead shone a round disc, like a mirror, or like the bright face of the moon, which indicated to me who she was. Vipers rising from the left and right supported this disc, with ears of grain sprouting beside them. Her multi-colored robe was made of the finest linen; part was gleaming white, part saffron-yellow, part glowing red. But what caught and held my gaze more than anything else was the deep black glossy mantle. She wore it slung across her body from the right hip to the left shoulder, where it was tied in a knot resembling a shield-boss; but part of it was draped in countless folds flowing gracefully to its lowest edge with tasseled fringes. Its hem was interwoven with twinkling stars and in their midst shone the breathing fire of the half moon. But wherever the sweep of that wonderful mantle stirred, it carried with it a garland intertwined of all kinds of flowers and fruit.
>
> The emblems she carried were of different kinds. In her right hand, she held a bronze rattle; its narrow rim was curved like a sword-belt and pierced horizontally through it were several slender rods, which sounded shrilly when she shook the handle three times. A gold dish in the shape of a boat hung from her left hand and along the upper surface of the handle an asp was writhing, with its throat puffed out and its head raised, ready to strike. On the goddess' feet were slippers made from palm-leaves, the symbol of victory.

The *nāvigium Īsidis* described in the students' textbook was celebrated every year, after the winter storms, at the beginning of the sailing season; it was performed not only at Alexandria, but wherever a temple of Isis was situated near the sea. A lively description of this colorful event is presented by Apuleius in his *Metamorphoses* XI.9–11 and 16–17, translated by Lewis and Reinhold II.576–77. The passion and resurrection of Osiris was also an annual festival. Juvenal *Satires* VI.532–41 and VIII.29–30, describes the crowd of devotees uttering cries of grief, running to and fro, and their exultant shouts when Osiris is found. Every spring, the birth of Horus was also celebrated.

Services were held daily at the first and eighth hours. They were conducted by white-robed priests and accompanied by music (pipes, sistra, and antiphonal choral singing). Liturgy, sacrifice, the sprinkling of holy water, and the revelation of a richly dressed statue of Isis, like a Mexican *Virgen*, all formed part of these services. Ask students to identify some of these features of the service pictured on p. 136 of Unit 2. The ibises in the foreground were not for sacrifice. They were there as either part of the Egyptian decor or as symbols of the goddess' power of healing. Sacrifices to Isis consisted of milk, honey, or herbs, never of animals or birds.

Sacramental meals and private meditation were also regarded as a means of achieving a state of unity with the godhead. In the Isaeum at Pompeii is a bench that may have been used for private meditation.

Nevertheless, despite its appeal to human emotion and widespread popularity at the beginning of the Empire, the cult of Isis was virtually dead by the fourth century A.D. The reasons were varied: initiation into the cult was expensive, the theology lacked philosophical rigor, and other Greek and Roman divinities were so easily accommodated into the cult that the worship of Isis lost its distinctive identity.

Suggestions for Discussion and Further Work

1 Which religious festivals are associated with public holidays in Canada and the United States today? Which of them are filled with fun, even rowdiness?
2 Describe a religious ceremony that you have seen or participated in, which had some kind of procession or drama in it.
3 After students have read the stories in this stage and discussed Isis and her worship, they might write a description of an Isiac service in Alexandria, at which Clemens was a spectator. Clemens should be the narrator, and the impressions of the service his.
4 Read extracts from the *Golden Ass* (tr. Graves, Penguin, Ch. 17 & 18), which deal specifically with Isis. Older students might read the entire work; it describes the picaresque adventures of the hero Lucius who converts, after many errors, to the Isiac religion. One of the characters in the work, viz. the baker's sadistic wife, may be a caricature of a Christian by a non-Christian author (Apuleius *Metamorphoses* IX.14–15).

STAGE 20: MEDICUS

BRIEF OUTLINE

Reading passages } medicine, pseudo-medicine, and science
Background material

Chief grammatical points   present participle
                           oblique cases of *is*

NARRATIVE POINTS

A.D. Date	Setting	Characters Introduced	Story Line
Flashback (cont.): Spring 81	Barbillus' estate on the Nile river	Petro (Greek doctor), Plotina (Barbillus' [deceased] wife), Rufus (their son)	Astrologer's superstitious cures are scorned by Petro. Barbillus tells Quintus how his wife and son sailed to Greece against advice of astrologer. Plotina drowned at sea; he disinherited Rufus, who is now in Roman army in Britain. Barbillus dies of astrologer's "cure," but first commissions Quintus to find Rufus and convey his final wish for a reconciliation with his son. Barbillus' will.

GRAMMATICAL POINTS

increased incidence of present participle
    e.g. *ancillae prope lectum stābant, lacrimantēs.*
increased incidence of oblique cases of *is*
    e.g. *Petrō, postquam dē vulnere Barbillī audīvit, statim ad vīllam eius festīnāvit.*
descriptive genitive
    e.g. *astrologus, quī in vīllā Barbillī habitābat, erat vir ingeniī prāvī.*
increased incidence of predicative adjective
    e.g. *subitō puerum vīdī in triviīs stantem.*

SENTENCE PATTERNS

increased complexity of sentence structure
(iii) "stringing" of two parallel subordinate clauses

Stage Commentaries

e.g. *servī, quī Barbillum portābant, ubi cubiculum intrāvērunt, in lectum eum lēniter posuērunt.*

Model Sentences

These sentences continue the story of Barbillus' injury, sustained in the last story of Stage 19. Barbillus is carried into the house; amidst the general hysteria, Phormio departs to the city, to find a doctor.

The sentences also introduce present participles, singular and plural, nominative case. Students have already met several examples in previous stages, but you should postpone detailed discussion of forms and uses of the present participle until the first language note, pp. 145–46.

The following words are new: *lectum* (new meaning), *medicum*.

remedium astrologī

Barbillus' shoulder is still bleeding as he is brought into the house, although Phormio has devised a sort of tourniquet from a piece of his own tunic. Phormio now suggests applying cobwebs (which do in fact contain a natural coagulant) to the wound to staunch the blood. The astrologer, meanwhile, is lamenting the fact that no one listened to his dire warnings; consulted on a remedy, he proposes a black mouse, killed, dissected, and placed on the wound. On overhearing this, Barbillus advises Quintus to seek Petro, "a good doctor." Quintus at once dispatches Phormio on this errand.

The astrologer, who in the last story of Stage 19 tried to dissuade Barbillus from hunting on an unpropitious day, now applies the remedy to his injured shoulder. He lives with Barbillus as a private horoscoper and member of the household. Numerous wealthy Romans kept such a person on their private staff, and referred various domestic and business matters to him for advice about whether the time was right for a particular course of action. Now the astrologer, claiming that his cures are effective, proposes a form of medical treatment, and he adopts an attitude of professional rivalry towards doctors. The practice of medicine at this time belonged to both the rational and the irrational world. Barbillus wants the best of both worlds. This story is recorded on the audio-cassette.

See Tacitus *Annals* VI.20–22 for the clever method by which the Emperor Tiberius tested the credentials of the astrologer Thrasyllus, and for the historian's reflections (ch. 22) on the credibility of the idea that the course of human events is predestined.

The picture on p. 141 of Unit 2 shows medical instruments made of bronze which were found at Pompeii. At the top are four different types of forceps; in the center, from left to right, are polyp forceps, scissors, possibly a lancet, a rasp probe, a bone forceps and small forceps; on the right are two scalpels; at the bottom are four types of flat probe. The variety suggests a range of surgical processes, as mentioned in the background material, pp. 154–59. For other pictures illustrating Roman medicine, see slides 21–23.

Some Suggested Questions

What kind of person is Phormio?
Why would Barbillus be more likely to trust the astrologer now than he was before the hunt? Is he completely in the astrologer's hands at this point?
Is the astrologer a crook? Or does he believe his own claims?
Who are the *Chaldaeī* (line 21)? Why does the astrologer mention them in particular? (Chaldaei are described in this Manual, p. 80 above.)
Whose ear is "my" ear (*in aurem meam*, line 26) into which Barbillus whispered, "Send for Petro, the good doctor"?

Petrō

Petro, a Greek doctor with an excellent local reputation, comes at Quintus' instigation and sets about applying the techniques of scientific medicine. His methods contrast sharply with those of the astrologer. He has surgical skill; he knows the importance of hygiene; and he understands that healing is a natural function. In this story science successfully opposes magic.

Some details of the operation performed by Petro may unsettle a squeamish student. Most students, however, seem untroubled or even positively enjoy them. Some may ask about the use of vinegar in this context. It is intended as an anesthetic and would also be of some value in the attempt to stop bleeding. See Majno 186–88, on wine and vinegar as antiseptics.

Some Suggested Questions

Was Petro right to be angry with the astrologer?
In what ways was Petro's treatment similar to modern medicine?
Which part of the treatment is being shown in the picture, p. 143? Quote the appropriate Latin. (Answer: *cutem . . . perītē cōnseruit*, lines 17–18)

Not surprisingly doctors attracted criticism and were the butt of popular jokes then as now. You might like to put these two epigrams of Martial (both of which come in Unit 4, Stage 36) on the blackboard and ask students to help with the translation.

Stage Commentaries

> *languebam; sed tu comitatus protinus ad me*
> *venisti centum, Symmache, discipulis.*
> *centum me tetigere manus Aquilone gelatae:*
> *non habui febrem, Symmache: nunc habeo.*   Martial V.9

> *nuper erat medicus, nunc est vespillo Diaulus:*
> *quod vespillo facit, fecerat et medicus.*   Martial I.47

For similar material in translation, see C.S.C.P. *The Roman World* Unit I, Item 62.

First Language Note (Present Participles)

When students have read this note and completed the exercises, follow up with oral drill, based on the Complete Vocabulary, pp. 198–213. Give the students present participles of unfamiliar verbs to translate, e.g. *arcessēns* or *arcessentēs* / *relinquēns* or *relinquentēs*, and allow them to look up e.g. *arcessō* or *relinquō* in the Complete Vocabulary to determine lexical meaning. (If students cannot figure out from hearing the participle how to spell it, write it on the blackboard; some students seem to learn only through the eye.) If time allows, give students infinitives and ask them to form the present nominative, singular and plural, participles—e.g. those in the checklists of Stages 18–20: *amāre, arcessere, audēre, caedere, castīgāre, cognōscere, collocāre, comparāre, cōnficere, cōnsistere, dēfendere, dēmōnstrāre, discēdere, equitāre, fluere, frangere, īnferre, irrumpere, līberāre, obstāre, persuādēre, petere* "beg for," *poscere, prōcumbere, recūsāre, relinquere, resistere, saevīre, temptāre, vīvere.* Note that two of the verbs (*obstāre* and *resistere*) take dative objects; see also previous list of verbs taking the dative in this Manual, p. 71 above.

fortūna crūdēlis

While nursing Barbillus, Quintus learns about his past life. A disagreement in Barbillus' family terminated the earlier happiness of his marriage. The trouble began when he consulted the astrologer about the wisdom of a proposed family visit to Athens; the warning this man gave undoubtedly sharpened the conflict which already existed to an extent between father and son. The adolescent Rufus then over-simplified an appeal to reason in order to justify doing what he already wanted to do, i.e. go to Athens for the wedding of an old school-friend, Eupor, with the result that Rufus' mother, who finally accompanied him on the journey without Barbillus, was drowned in a shipwreck. After this, Barbillus did not wish to see his son again, and Rufus, reluctantly complying with his father's wishes, eventually went to Britain and signed up with the Roman army there.

Stage 20

Students who are themselves adolescents will probably recognize the situation leading to the conflict, but may also identify entirely with Rufus. If so, explore their views with them by asking whether they think Rufus' expressed reason for proceeding with the planned trip (*astrologī nōn sunt nautae*, lines 22–23) was adequate. Do they see the problem only in terms of the rational logic of the son opposed to the superstitious anxiety of the father? Or do they think there were other considerations that Rufus should have kept in mind? Do they approve of the mother Plotina's acquiescence to her son's will? Can they infer why she acquiesced?

If some students ask about *ad lītus* (line 28), wondering why it is not *ad lītum*, you could (*after* the story has been translated) refer them to the note on neuters in the Review Grammar, p. 163.

astrologus victor

The astrologer, who lives in Barbillus' house, takes advantage of his proximity to the sick man by constantly denigrating Petro's skill as a doctor. Barbillus, however, continues to trust the doctor until the astrologer tells him of a dream in which he claims to have discovered the secret of a cure for him. At this point, Barbillus relents, and permits the astrologer to administer a remedy which, in fact, hastens his demise. He barely has time to summon Quintus and entrust to him a conciliatory letter to Rufus, whom he enjoins Quintus to seek in Britain. Quintus insists, in spite of Barbillus' protests, on summoning the doctor, but by the time Petro arrives, it is too late. Barbillus has died.

Now the tables are turned. Barbillus cannot in the end free himself from the power of magic, and the astrologer wins him over eventually by playing on his belief in the interpretation of dreams. The pathos in the death of Barbillus, though reminiscent of the death of Caecilius at the end of Unit 1, is intended to be more mature and to touch on deeper emotional levels. There are no heroics; only the sadness of wisdom that comes too late. Barbillus' final gesture is one of reparation for his failure to forgive and to put away bitterness.

The picture on p. 149 shows a papyrus letter from Prokleios to Pekysis, first century A.D. from Alexandria. The letter reads: "Prokleios to his good friend Pekysis, greetings. You will do well if at your own risk you sell to my friend Sotas such high-quality goods as he will tell you he needs, for him to bring to me at Alexandria. Know that you will have to deal with me about the cost. Greet all your family from me. Farewell."

Some Suggested Questions

Why should Barbillus, an apparently sensible and intelligent man, believe in astrology? Do you find such behavior credible? (Remind students that in antiquity astrology had the status virtually of a religion; and that the astrologer of the stories correctly foresaw the danger of the crocodile hunt in Stage 19, "vēnātiō," and of sailing to Athens in late autumn in "fortūna crūdēlis" in the present stage.)

What is it about astrology that you might regard as not sensible? How might an astrologer ensure that his advice seemed reliable or at least plausible?

What is Quintus' attitude towards astrology? Do you think his attitude would have changed as a result of Barbillus' tragedy?

Why do you think Barbillus refused to let Quintus send again for Petro?

What might the letter (entrusted to Quintus) for Rufus have contained?

For grammatical work, review nouns, particularly those in the more recent stages, viz. Stages 18–20. Begin by asking students to pick out, in the stories, nouns that are described (1) by an adjective, (2) a genitive phrase, or (3) a relative clause. Once the student has isolated such a noun, the description—whichever its three forms—should help him or her translate its lexical meaning. Ask for the noun's gender (especially if it is a 3rd declension noun) or for its case or for its number. Often the descriptive adjective, genitive, or relative clause will help the student to determine these variables. If students have difficulty with a particular noun, write (or choose a student "secretary" to write) a mini-paradigm (usually excluding the ablative), singular and plural, of the noun on the blackboard. Needless to say, these paradigms of difficult nouns should also find their way into the students' grammar notebooks.

Below is a selection of nouns in the checklists of Stages 18–20:

1st declension nouns, feminine: *fortūna, lūna, pompa, stola.*

2nd declension nouns, masculine: *locus, medicus, oculus, umerus.*

2nd declension nouns, neuter: *perīculum, praesidium, remedium.*

3rd declension nouns, feminine: *ars, artis; auris, auris; hiems, hiemis; mors, mortis; nox, noctis; parēns, parentis* (also m.); *pars, partis; vōx, vōcis.*

3rd declension nouns, masculine: *mīles, mīlitis; parēns, parentis* (also f.); *sermō, sermōnis.*

3rd declension nouns, neuter: *caput, capitis; iter, itineris; vulnus, vulneris.*

4th declension nouns: *domus, domūs* f.; *manus, manūs* f.; *sonitus, sonitūs* m.

After drilling these nouns as suggested above, assign the list (or with younger students, part of it) as home-study for a quiz the next day. On the quiz, students might write the appropriate form of *bonus* after each noun in order to show that they know its gender.

Stage 20

Second Language Note (Oblique Cases of is)

When students have studied this note, consolidate the oblique forms of *is* inside a paradigm matrix, either by writing the forms in the proper positions as they come up in the sentences or by referring students to p. 177 of the Review Grammar. The mini-paradigm (usually excluding ablatives and all neuter forms) should also find its way into the pronoun section of the students' grammar notebooks (if it is not already there).

Drills and Suggestions for Further Practice

Exercise 1 Type: translation
          Grammatical point being practiced: relative clause

Encourage idiomatic English equivalents for the Latin relative clause. Watch for evidence of students' inability to determine the beginning or, more probably, the ending of the clause. Although the punctuation should help, some students ignore boundaries and markers and hence distort the meaning of the sentence. However, if you read aloud properly and the class choruses your Latin, students will have less trouble determining clause boundaries. In the later stages of the students' textbook, the frequent use of commas to mark clause boundaries decreases, and reading aloud properly will become even more helpful.

Exercise 2 Type: comprehension
There are extant Latin wills, and in style this exercise is based on them. The editors have attempted to make it look like an actual document, although in the interests of students' comprehension they have not reproduced ancient script and they have added punctuation. They have represented it as a document on papyrus, like many wills found in Egypt, but elsewhere where papyrus was less plentiful, wax tablets were used. For the sealing of documents, remind students of Stage 4 "Hermogenēs" and "in basilicā."

The exercise includes further practice of the relative clause and of the dative. Encourage students to give particulars in their answers to question 9: Barbillus might be called "realistic," "truthful," "fair rather than generous," etc. Encourage discussion, not only with the questions in the textbook, but also with others:

> How do we know that Barbillus completely trusted Quintus?
>   (Answer: He assumed that Quintus would carry out a faithful
>   search for Rufus, even though that was not in Quintus' interests.)
> How can we tell that the will was drawn up at least in its final form,
>   only a short time before Barbillus' death?
> How many of the signatories were Roman citizens?

Stage Commentaries

From one of the stories in this stage, ask students to pick out and identify examples of particular cases of nouns and/or adjectives, in the way described above on p. 90, but now including examples of the genitive and dative cases. Then with the aid of the paradigm in the Review Grammar, pp. 162–63, ask some volunteers to make up an English sentence which in Latin would have contained *servōrum* (or *cīvēs*, *urbī*, *puellīs*, etc.). This drill is less difficult than it sounds, and although lack of knowledge will inevitably produce some mistakes (e.g. the suggestion "We went to the city" for *urbī*), it can be an effective reminder to students of the functions of the cases.

The Background Material

This stage develops the theme of medicine and pseudo-medicine. Should the short account of Greek medical science given in Unit 2 not be sufficient for satisfying students' curiosity, you could find more detail in Beaujeau, "Medicine," in Taton 341–68; C.S.C.P. *The Romans discover Britain*, pp. 46–47 (translated source material) and the Teacher's Handbook; Scarborough; Singer.

If students want to know more about the Alexandrian scholar-scientists, they might consult Beaujeau, "Astronomy and Mathematical Geography," in Taton 305–30; Lee; Majno; Sarton. Particularly interesting are the calculations and inventions of Aristarchus, Eratosthenes, Archimedes, Ctesibius, and Hero. Read aloud Evans 143–52—excellent passages on medicine and science in antiquity.

Suggestions for Further Work

1 Discuss some modern applications for the following devices that were used by the Greeks and Romans: (a) pulley; (b) lever; (c) concave mirror; (d) cog wheels.

When students have made their suggestions, extemporaneously or the next day after some research, refer them to Archimedes and his devices for defending Syracuse (Plutarch *Marcellus* 15–18; Livy XXIV.34). One or two volunteers, after further research, might report on Archimedes to the class. They should not omit the two anecdotes about his discovery of the principle of displacement, and his death.

2 Assign oral reports on Alexandrian scholar-scientists and their computations and discoveries: besides Archimedes, Aristarchus of Samos (heliocentric theory), Conon of Samos (conic sections), Ctesibius (elasticity of air), Erasistratus (circulation of blood), Eratosthenes (earth's circumference), Hero (steam-powered turbine; area of triangle), and Herophilus (dissection of human bodies).

3 Ask students to draw some of the "gadgets" invented by Alexandrian

scholars and explain how they worked. Discuss why Hero's "steam turbine," say, qualifies as a gadget instead of, as did Watts' turbine, a true engine.
4 Some students become fascinated with astrology. A volunteer group might research the mechanics of drawing up a horoscope and describe, with appropriate illustrations, their findings to the class.

The Language Information Section

This section, like the corresponding section for Unit 1, contains the two parts called "Review Grammar" and "Complete Vocabulary." New to this section, however, is a third part called the "Reference Grammar," which will be found between the Review Grammar and the Complete Vocabulary.

Part One: Review Grammar (pp. 162–89) is intended as a review section to be studied by students only after they have completed (or nearly completed) the Unit. Students should begin work in the Review Grammar soon after they have reached Stage 19, postponing those sections which review Stages 19 and 20 until after they have finished the stages. Although all the forms and the rules of sentence structure in Unit 2 are described briefly, the Review Grammar gives priority to numerous examples so that students can see the rules illustrated as well as described. Often, manipulation exercises are appended so that students can test their ability to apply the rules.

Part Two: Reference Grammar (pp. 190–97) presents complete paradigms of the grammar encountered in Unit 2 (including some forms not yet learned). It is designed for older or more able students who may appreciate a bird's eye view of the grammar to be presented in Unit 2 and are capable of getting a sense of what the Latin in the Unit will be like. Do not confuse this sense of the language, however, with the actual mastery of it; mastery comes only with time and practice of language in context, followed by the consolidation which the Review Grammar—not the Reference Grammar—provides. The Reference Grammar also contains longer and more formal descriptions of the rules of sentence structures in Unit 2 and a list of the Latin sentence patterns introduced in the Unit. These should be studied by students who are able enough to benefit from the more formal analysis of language after they have successfully completed work on the Stages and Review Grammar.

Part Three: Complete Vocabulary (pp. 198–213), contains all the words in Unit 2 and in the "Words and Phrases Checklists" in Unit 1 with their meanings. Its format is explained in the notes which preface this part (p. 198). Emphasize paragraph 1, which describes the new layout for nouns (e.g. pāx, pācis, f. *peace*), and paragraph 3, which describes the new layout for verbs (e.g. āmittō, āmittere, āmīsī *lose*).

The comments following are concerned with individual sub-sections of the Language Information Section.

PART ONE: Review Grammar

Nouns (pp. 162–66). When students are working on the transformation exercises in paragraph 2 and 3 of this sub-section, emphasize the link between a word's ending and its function in the sentence. Have individual students read out and translate each sentence in its entirety both before and after the singular-to-plural or plural-to-singular transformation—though you may occasionally want to relax this rule to speed up the pace. If students have difficulty handling the 3rd declension nouns, show them how to consult the table of nouns in paragraph 1 and (when necessary) the entry for the relevant noun in the Complete Vocabulary.

Adjectives (pp. 167–68). The class might discuss the examples in paragraph 4. Students might suggest why they chose a particular inflection.

Comparison of Adjectives (pp. 169–71). Drill the transformations in paragraph 8 orally. For example, after a student has completed sentence 3a, ask, "What is the superlative form of *fortiōrēs*?"

Pronouns (pp. 172–77). The terms "relative pronoun" and "antecedent" are introduced in paragraph 7. Ask students to pick out examples of relative pronouns and antecedents from a story read previously, in addition to the examples in paragraphs 7 or 11 (sentences 2, 4, 7, 9, 10, and 11). The term "demonstrative pronoun" is introduced in paragraphs 8 and 9; "determinative pronoun," in paragraph 10. If necessary, explain that the demonstrative pronoun implies a pointing gesture on the part of the speaker, whereas a determinative pronoun specifies gender without necessarily implying a pointing gesture.

Regular Verbs (pp. 178–81). Charted are models for the present, imperfect, perfect, and pluperfect tenses, as well as their infinitive and imperative forms. The present participle, described in Stage 20 (p. 145), is not included here, but will be discussed and practiced at length, together with the perfect participle, in the Unit 3 LI Section. In the meantime, students who are curious about them will find complete models for the present participles of all conjugations in the Reference Grammar, Section IV, p. 193.

Ask students to look at the verb charts in paragraph 1 and to answer questions like the following:

> In the present tense chart, look at the vowels *before* the personal endings. What are the similarities between the stem-vowels of the 3rd regular and "-*iō*" and 4th conjugations?
> In the imperfect tense chart, look at the endings *and* the vowels before them. How many sub-groups of endings are patterned among the five conjugations? (Answer: only three: -*ābam*, -*ēbam*, and -*iēbam*)

Language Information Section

In the imperfect tense chart, look at the endings *and* the letter immediately preceding. In which conjugation does a vowel precede the ending; in which, a consonant? In those with a vowel preceding, which conjugations have a long vowel; which, a short vowel?

In the pluperfect tense chart, look at the endings which follow the perfect stem. How does one use the perfect chart to determine the perfect stem? Is it true to say that the endings, taken together, are exactly the forms of *eram* (imperfect of *sum*)? (If students are unsure, refer them to paragraph 1 of the sub-section "Irregular Verbs.")

Irregular Verbs (pp. 182–84). In paragraph 1, students will find models for the present tense of *sum, possum, volō, eō,* and *ferō*, together with their imperfect and perfect forms (excluding the forms of *fuī*, the perfect of *sum*, which the students have not yet met). In paragraph 2, the forms of *volō* and *nōlō* are contrasted; in paragraph 3, the forms of *eram* and *poteram*; in paragraph 7, the forms of *sum, adsum,* and *absum*. If students ask about the imperfect of *nōlō* (not given in paragraph 1), explain that it has endings like those of *volō*: *nōlēbam* and *volēbam, nōlēbās* and *volēbās*, etc.

Word Order (pp. 184–85). Make up further examples of the patterns in paragraphs 1 (verb first) and 4 (accusative first). They are relatively frequent in original Latin literature. Of the examples in paragraph 6, students have met the pattern dative + accusative + verb (sentences 1 and 2) from Stage 16 onwards; dative + verb (sentences 3 and 4) from Stage 17 onwards.

Longer Sentences I (pp. 186–88). In the sentences of paragraphs 1–6, the subordinate clauses vary in four ways:

(a) they are introduced by a variety of conjunctions;
(b) their subject is sometimes the same as the subject of the main clause, and sometimes different;
(c) they sometimes precede the main clause, sometimes follow it, and sometimes interrupt it;
(d) they include various additional complexities such as the prolate infinitive, the predicative use of the adjective, and the patterns dative + verb and dative + accusative + verb.

The exercise in paragraph 6 is fairly demanding. Help younger or otherwise less able students translate orally in class the clauses and perhaps the sentences before assigning the matching as group work or as homework. For sentence 5, in its completed form, lead students to the translation "After the mother . . . ." rather than "The mother, after she . . . ."

After students have studied paragraphs 7 and 8, ask them, "How can you tell where a relative clause begins and ends?" If they reply, "By the commas," ask them, "Could you still tell the beginning and the end without commas?" After looking again, students might observe that the clauses begin with a form of *quī* (relative pronoun) and end with a verb. If so, confirm that this is the usual, though not invariable, pattern. Ask also how Latin sentences containing relative clauses should be read aloud—with or without pauses before and after? If the students cannot answer, ask them to read aloud sentences 2, 4, 6, 8, and 10 in paragraph 8. Why ought the relative clauses in these sentences be read without pauses before and after? Why didn't the editors set these relative clauses off with commas? If time allows, write on the blackboard, from the stories elsewhere in the students' textbook, some sentences with non-restrictive relative clauses and compare them with sentences here in paragraph 8. Unless students are older, however, do not introduce the technical terms "restrictive" and "non-restrictive." Allow students to describe the difference in their own words.

Longer Sentences II (p. 189). This sub-section begins with examples where a verb in the first of two parallel clauses has to be supplied in the second; it continues with the harder (but more typically Latin) pattern in which a verb in the second clause must be supplied in the first. Read the sentences aloud, with careful phrasing, to help students grasp the meaning.

PART TWO: Reference Grammar

The models of nouns, adjectives, pronouns, and verbs charted in Sections I–IV (pp. 190–93) contain forms which the students will not have met, unless they have studied some Latin from textbooks which have an order of grammatical presentation different from that in this course. Refer younger students to these full charts, if they are curious about the "blanks" (i.e. "not yet learned" notations) in the charts of the Review Grammar (pp. 162–89), but do not confuse them by forcing them to memorize at this time the forms which they do not meet in the readings of Unit 2. But allow older students, if they wish and can, to save time by memorizing the anticipatory forms when they first see them here.

The descriptions of syntax in Sections V–IX (pp. 193–95) are provided largely for the benefit of older or extremely able students who can think about a language as well as comprehend it.

Complementary and subject infinitives are described in Section V. If students have difficulty understanding the infinitive as subject, point out that English is more likely to use an "-ing" verbal (i.e. gerund) in similar contexts, e.g. "Resisting is useless."

Advise older students that the constructions described in Sections VII ("Relative Clauses"), VIII ("Participial Phrases"), and IX.2 ("Genitive

Language Information Section

of Description") often serve as longer variations of an adjective modifying a noun, as described in Section VI ("Agreement of Nouns and Adjectives"). For example, in English, we may talk about a "strong person," "a person who is strong," "a person, being strong," or "a person of strength." Although the meaning stays more or less the same, the expression can change for reasons of style or emphasis in English as in Latin.

Section X (p. 196) will repay careful study by students of all ages, although younger students may take longer—with the teacher providing more examples than are found in this section—to learn the mechanics and concept of principal parts. Students who know the principal parts of at least the most common verbs are more likely to recognize the lexical meaning of discrete forms, e.g. *tulī* as belonging to the system of *ferō* ("bring"). Once students have learned the infinitive in Stages 13 and 14, begin quizzing them orally and in writing on the principal parts of common verbs. You will find the first three principal parts after most verb entries in the Complete Vocabulary (pp. 198–213). Be prepared to give the fourth principal part (if there is one) of a verb, but only if a student asks about it. Do not dwell on it, as perfect participles are taught in Stages 21 and 22 at the beginning of Unit 3. Take the age and ability of your students as your guide in deciding on the number of verbs for which you will teach the first three principal parts. And if you distribute lists of principal parts for study by the students, go ahead and include all the principal parts on the list, though you need not (generally should not) assign the fourth part for memorization at this point. Soon, when students have gone on to Unit 3, they will be able to use these same lists to study the fourth principal part, the perfect participle.

Experience shows that some students, especially young ones, need considerable experience and help in deducing the vocabulary-entry, or present-tense form, of a verb when only the perfect form appears in a given sentence or story. In the Complete Vocabulary, forms that look very different from the entry form are given a cross reference (e.g. *cecidī* see *cadō*). Forms that are quite like their entry form are not given separate entries (e.g. the text may have *admīsit* and the student must deduce *admittō* to find it in the Complete Vocabulary). This problem may become particularly acute if students are not given practice in "backforming" a present-tense form from the perfect. You might, therefore, when drilling principal parts orally, drill them "backwards" from the perfect, through the infinitive, to the present (e.g. *cecidī*, *cadere*, *cadō*) as well as "forwards" (e.g. *cadō*, *cadere*, *cecidī*). This kind of activity is best when prescribed in small doses, but frequently.

PART THREE: Complete Vocabulary

Spend a little time helping the class to study the notes (p. 198) which introduce this part; otherwise, they may misunderstand and/or misuse the vocabulary which follows (pp. 199–213). Ask individual students to look up a word and then interpret aloud, for the benefit of the other students, the notations after a noun (i.e. genitive form and gender marking) or a verb (first three principal parts). Also, while students are translating stories in the stages themselves, appoint a "secretary" for the class or for each group, whose duty it will be to look up problematic words and explain the information, other than the English meaning, which the Complete Vocabulary provides after many entries.

Other Aids

Make students aware very early in the course of the study aids included at the back of their textbooks, the "Guide to Characters and Places" (pp. 214–16), "Index of Cultural Topics" (p. 217), "Index of Grammatical Topics" (pp. 218–19), and "Time Chart" (pp. 220–22). All of these will become increasingly useful when students try to consolidate their knowledge of Unit 2 at review or examination time.

Diagnostic Tests

For a discussion of the purpose of the diagnostic tests, and suggestions for their use, see the Unit 1 Teacher's Manual, p. 110. The words and phrases in bold face are either new to students or have occurred infrequently in the reading material up to the stage indicated.

Test 4

To be given at the end of Stage 16.

somnium mīrābile
    Sextus et Titus erant amīcī. ad urbem **iter faciēbant**. postquam ad urbem pervēnērunt, Sextus ad tabernam contendit. Titus tamen apud frātrem manēbat. post cēnam Titus, quod fessus erat, mox obdormīvit. subitō Sextus in **somniō** appāruit et clāmāvit,
    "amīce! caupō mē necāre vult. necesse est tibi mē **adiuvāre**."   5
    Titus statim surrēxit, quod **commōtus** erat, et sibi dīxit,
    "num caupō amīcum meum necāre vult? minimē! somnium erat."
    Titus iterum obdormīvit. Sextus iterum in somniō appāruit et clāmāvit,
    "ēheu! mortuus sum. caupō **scelestus** mē necāvit. postquam mē   10
necāvit, in plaustrō mē **cēlāvit**. tū eum pūnīre dēbēs."
    Titus ē lectō perterritus surrēxit et **vigilēs** petīvit. vigilibus rem nārrāvit. tum cum duōbus vigilibus ad tabernam contendit. caupōnem rogāvit,
    "ubi est Sextus, amīcus meus, quī in hāc tabernā manēbat?"   15
    "**errōrem** facis," caupō eī respondit. "**nēmō** est in tabernā."
    Titus, ubi plaustrum in viā cōnspexit, clāmāvit,
    "ecce! amīcus meus, quem tū necāvistī, in hōc plaustrō **cēlātus** est."
    vigilēs, postquam plaustrum īnspexērunt, Sextum invēnērunt   20
mortuum. caupōnem attonitum **comprehendērunt**, et eum ad iūdicem dūxērunt.

On *vigilibus rem nārrāvit* (lines 12–13) see note on Stage 16 exercise 2, p. 51 above.

Test 5

To be given at the end of Stage 18, preferably in two successive lessons.

ad pȳramidas

(a) Translate

ōlim Quīntus ad tabernam Clēmentis contendit. ubi ad tabernam
pervēnit, Clēmentem salūtāvit.
"salvē, amīce," inquit. "ego tibi aliquid dīcere volō. ad
pȳramidas iter facere cupiō. sunt enim in Aegyptō multae
pȳramides quās Aegyptiī ōlim **exstrūxērunt**. Aegyptiī in 5
pȳramidibus rēgēs **sepelīre** solēbant. ego pȳramidas vidēre volō
quod sunt maximae et pulcherrimae. vīsne mēcum iter facere?"
    Clēmēns laetus cōnsēnsit. itaque Quīntus et Clēmēns pecūniam et
cibum in **saccīs** posuērunt. tum ad Plūtum, mercātōrem Graecum,
festīnāvērunt et **camēlōs condūxērunt**. saccōs, quōs ē tabernā 10
Clēmentis portāverant, in camēlīs posuērunt. tum camēlōs
cōnscendērunt et ex urbe discessērunt. per agrōs et vīllās
prōcēdēbant.
    subitō decem Aegyptiī, quī **īnsidiās** parāverant, impetum
fēcērunt. Quīntus et Clēmēns fortiter resistēbant sed facile erat 15
Aegyptiīs eōs superāre quod fūstēs ingentēs habēbant. tum Aegyptiī
cum pecūniā et camēlīs effūgērunt. Quīntus et Clēmēns trīstēs ad
urbem reveniēbant.
    "ēheu!" inquit Clēmēns. "quam miserī sumus! pȳramidas nōn
vīdimus: pecūniam et camēlōs āmīsimus." 20

(b) Read the rest of the story and, without translating, answer the
questions at the end.

Quīntus et Clēmēns per urbem fessī prōcēdēbant. ubi tabernam
Plūtī praeterībant, rem mīrābilem vīdērunt. camēlī, quōs Aegyptiī
abdūxerant, **extrā** tabernam Plūtī stābant! tum Quīntus rem
tōtam intellēxit. amīcī īrātī mercātōrem quaesīvērunt, sed invenīre
nōn poterant. aderat tamen puer parvus quī camēlōs custōdiēbat. 25
Quīntus puerō clāmāvit,
    "heus, tū! ubi sunt Aegyptiī quī in nōs impetum fēcērunt? ego
eōs dē pecūniā meā **interrogāre** volō."
    puer perterritus "rogā Plūtum," inquit, et statim fūgit.
    amīcī per viās Alexandrīae Plūtum frūstrā quaesīvērunt. tandem 30
thermās intrāvērunt. ecce! Plūtus in palaestrā cum **duōbus** servīs
ambulābat. Quīntus servōs agnōvit. eōs enim vīderat in turbā
Aegyptiōrum quī impetum fēcerant. Quīntus ad Plūtum prōcessit,

Diagnostic Tests

 quī, postquam eum īrātum vīdit, valdē timēbat. Quīntus clāmāvit,
"ubi est mea pecūnia? camēlōs iam invēnimus!"   35
 Plūtus erat perterritus quod Quīntus erat cīvis Rōmānus. Plūtus
Quīntō "**ignōsce** mihi," inquit. "ego tibi pecūniam libenter reddō et
parvum dōnum tibi offerō."
 deinde Quīntum et Clēmentem ad vīllam suam dūxit. ibi eīs duōs
equōs dedit. Quīntus numquam equōs pulchriōrēs quam illōs   40
vīderat! tum Quīntus et Clēmēns equōs cōnscendērunt et ad
pȳramidas laetī contendērunt.

1 How were Quintus and Clemens feeling when they got back to the city?
2 How did they know they were on the track of the thieves?
3 What question did Quintus ask the boy?
4 What did the boy reply?
5 Where was Plutus and what was he doing when Quintus and Clemens found him?
6 What did Quintus notice about the slaves attending Plutus?
7 Why was Plutus so frightened when Quintus told him about the camels?
8 What happened when Plutus took Quintus and Clemens to his house?
9 What did Quintus think of Plutus' present?
10 How does the story end?

Test 6

To be given at the end of Stage 20, preferably in two successive lessons.

testāmentum Barbillī

(a) Translate

multī amīcī cum Galatēā et Aristōne cēnābant. dē morte Barbillī
colloquium habēbant.
 "magnum **lēgātum** exspectō," inquit Galatēa. "nam ubi
Barbillus aeger iacēbat, eum cotīdiē vīsitābam. magnam partem diēī
cum eō **cōnsūmēbam**."   5
 omnēs Galatēam laudāvērunt et clāmāvērunt,
 "decōrum est tibi praemium **meritum** accipere."
 Petrō, medicus Graecus, triclīnium intrāvit. Galatēa, ubi eum
cōnspexit, īrāta surrēxit et rogāvit,
 "cūr hūc vēnistī? nōs omnēs tē **dēspicimus**, quod tū Barbillum 10
sānāre nōn poterās."
 "ego hūc vēnī, quod tibi aliquid dīcere volō," respondit Petrō.

"quid est?" rogāvit Galatēa.
"**testāmentum** Barbillī vīdī," respondit ille.
Galatēa, ubi hoc audīvit, **īram dēposuit**. Petrōnem in mediōs 15
amīcōs dūxit et cibum vīnumque eī obtulit.
"ō **dulcissime**," inquit Galatēa, "quam libenter tē vidēmus. **dīc**
nōbīs quam celerrimē dē testāmentō! quid Barbillus nōbīs relīquit?"

(b) Read the rest of the story and, without translating, answer the
questions at the end.

omnēs tacuērunt et Petrōnem intentē audīvērunt.
"Barbillus Aristōnī nūllam pecūniam relīquit," inquit Petrō, "sed 20
tragoediās, quās Aristō scrīpsit, reddidit."
amīcī statim rīsērunt quod tragoediae Aristōnis pessimae erant.
Galatēa quoque rīsit.
"optimē fēcit Barbillus," inquit Galatēa. "Barbillus Aristōnī
tragoediās **sōlum** relīquit quod Aristō nihil aliud cūrat. **sine dubiō** 25
Barbillus mihi multam pecūniam relīquit quod ego **prūdentior** sum
quam marītus meus."
tum Petrō Galatēae dīxit, "Barbillus fīliae tuae gemmās, quās ā
mercātōre Arabī ēmit, relīquit."
"quam fortūnāta est Helena!" exclāmāvērunt amīcī. 30
Galatēa hanc rem graviter ferēbat.
"nōn decōrum est Helenae gemmās habēre. nam Helena est
stultior quam pater. **tūtius est** Helenae gemmās mihi trādere. sed
cūr nihil dē mē dīcis, Petrō? quid Barbillus mihi relīquit?"
Petrō tamen nihil respondit. 35
"dīc mihi, stultissime," inquit Galatēa īrāta.
tandem Petrō susurrāvit, "nihil tibi relīquit."
omnēs amīcī valdē commōtī erant: multī cachinnāvērunt, paucī
lacrimāvērunt.
Galatēa tamen tacēbat. **humī** dēciderat exanimāta. 40

1 What did Aristo receive in the will?
2 What did Galatea's friends do when they heard what Aristo had received?
3 What, according to Galatea, was Aristo's only interest in life?
4 What did Galatea hope to receive herself?
5 Why did Galatea's friends describe Helena as "fortūnāta"?
6 Why is the Arab merchant mentioned?
7 What does Galatea think about her daughter's character?
8 What does she think her daughter should do?
9 From Petro's behavior at the end of the story, find two reasons for supposing that he was embarrassed about telling Galatea what she had received.

Diagnostic Tests

10 What did Galatea receive?
11 How did most of Galatea's friends show their feelings about this? How did a few of them behave?
12 What effect did the news have on Galatea?

Part (a) of this test can be used to assess, among other things, the students' ability to handle the 1st and 2nd person inflections of the verb in various tenses. You may also wish to note how they cope with the omission of the subject in *Petrōnem . . . dūxit et cibum . . . obtulit* (lines 15–16).

If pupils produce "the will which Barbillus has left us" for line 18, discussion of the punctuation of the Latin may give them a clearer understanding of where they went wrong than analysis of the difference between "quid" and "quod."

Vocabulary tested in part (b) includes *rīdēre* (cf. question 2), *nihil aliud* (question 3), *emere* (question 6) and *cachinnāre* (question 11). In answering question 9, students have not only to understand the text but also to draw inferences from it; such exploration of the text could be taken further in oral discussion after the test has been completed. For example, the class might be asked to pick out, and suggest explanations for Galatea's change of tone from "*ō dulcissime*" in line 17 of part (a) to "*dīc mihi, stultissime*" in line 36 of part (b).

Appendix A: Cumulated List of Checklist Words

The number in parentheses refers to the stage in which the word appears in the checklist.

a
ā, ab (= from) (17)
abesse (6)
abīre (10)
accipere (10)
ad (3)
adesse (5)
adīre (20)
advenīre (13)
aedificāre (16)
aedificium (13)
aeger (13)
agere (4)
agitāre (8)
agmen (15)
agnōscere (9)
agricola (5)
aliquid (18)
alius (15)
alter (13)
amāre (19)
ambulāre (5)
amīcus (2)
āmittere (12)
ancilla (2)
animus (17)
antīquus (14)
ānulus (4)
appropinquāre (17)
apud (14)
aqua (15)
āra (17)
arcessere (20)
argenteus (14)
ars (20)
ātrium (1)
attonitus (14)
audēre (18)
audīre (5)
aula (14)
auris (20)
auxilium (16)
avārus (6)

b
bene (17)
benignus (17)
bibere (3)
bonus (16)

c
caedere (19)
callidus (10)
canis (1)
cantāre (13)
capere (10)
caput (18)
cārus (19)
castīgāre (19)
cautē (19)
celebrāre (9)
celeriter (9)
cēna (2)
cēnāre (7)
centuriō (7)
cēra (4)
cēterī (13)
cibus (2)
cinis (12)
circumspectāre (3)
cīvis (9)
clāmāre (3)
clāmor (5)
claudere (15)
coepisse (18)
cōgitāre (19)
cognōscere (18)
collocāre (20)
commodus (15)
comparāre (19)
complēre (12)
cōnficere (19)
coniūrātiō (13)
cōnsentīre (16)
cōnsilium (16)
cōnsistere (18)
cōnspicere (7)
cōnsūmere (8)
contendere (5)
contentus (10)
convenīre (11)
coquere (4)
coquus (1)
cotīdiē (14)
crēdere (11)
crūdēlis (20)
cubiculum (6)
cum (= with) (7)
cupere (9)
cūr? (4)
cūrāre (19)
currere (5)
custōdīre (12)
custōs (13)

d

dare (9)
dē (= about) (11)
dē (= down from) (19)
dea (18)
dēbēre (15)
decem (20)
dēcidere (13)
decōrus (14)
dēfendere (19)
deinde (16)
dēlectāre (16)
dēlēre (14)
dēmōnstrāre (18)
dēnique (20)
dēnsus (12)
dērīdēre (16)
dēsilīre (17)
dēspērāre (17)
deus (14)
dīcere (13)
dictāre (14)
diēs (9)
diēs nātālis (9)
difficilis (14)
dīligenter (14)
dīmittere (16)
discēdere (18)
diū (17)
doctus (20)
domina (14)
dominus (2)
domus (20)
dōnum (14)
dormīre (2)
dūcere (8)
dulcis (19)
duo (12 & 20)

e

ē (4)
ecce! (3)
effigiēs (15)
effugere (16)
ego (4)
ēheu! (4)
emere (6)
ēmittere (9)
epistula (12)
equitāre (20)
equus (15)
esse (1)
et (3)
etiam (15)
euge! (5)
eum (8)
exanimātus (17)
excitāre (13)
exclāmāre (10)
exercēre (9)
exīre (3)
exspectāre (3)

f

faber (16)
fābula (5)
fābulam agere (5)
facere (7)
facile (8)
facilis (17)
familiāris (14)
favēre (11)
fēmina (5)
ferōciter (6)
ferōx (8)
ferre (9)
fessus (13)
festīnāre (6)
fidēlis (14)
fīlia (19)
fīlius (1)
flamma (12)
flōs (16)
fluere (19)
fortasse (18)
forte (19)
fortis (6)
fortiter (12)
fortūna (18)
forum (3)
fossa (15)
frāctus (15)
frangere (18)
frāter (10)
frūmentum (16)
frūstrā (12)
fugere (12)
fulgēre (17)
fundus (12)
fūr (6)

g

geminī (13)
gemma (17)
gēns (11)
gladius (8)
grātiās agere (19)
graviter (17)
gustāre (2)

h

habēre (4)
habitāre (8)
haerēre (17)
hasta (17)
haurīre (13)
hercle! (10)
heri (7)
hic (8)
hiems (20)
hodiē (5)
homō (9)
honōrāre (15)
horreum (13)
hortus (1)
hospes (9)
hūc (17)

i

iacēre (12)
iam (12)
iānua (3)

ibi (18)
igitur (12)
ignāvus (8)
ille (9)
illūc (19)
impedīre (15)
imperātor (16)
imperium (10)
impetus (17)
in (1)
incidere (12)
incitāre (8)
īnfāns (6)
īnferre (20)
ingēns (7)
inimīcus (10)
inquit (4)
īnspicere (9)
īnsula (17)
intellegere (7)
intentē (6)
inter (16)
interficere (13)
intrāre (2)
invenīre (10)
invītāre (11)
invītus (18)
ipse (14)
īrātus (3)
īre (10)
irrumpere (20)
iste (14)
ita (16)
ita vērō (13)
itaque (17)
iter (19)
iterum (9)
iūdex (4)
iuvenis (5)

l
labōrāre (1)
lacrimāre (7)
laetus (2)

latrō (17)
lātus (20)
laudāre (2)
lavāre (14)
lectus (15)
legere (11)
lentē (15)
leō (3)
libenter (18)
liber (10)
līberālis (11)
līberāre (20)
lībertus (6)
lītus (15)
locus (19)
longus (18)
lūna (20)

m
magnus (3)
māne (19)
manēre (9)
manus (= hand) (18)
mare (17)
marītus (14)
māter (1)
maximus (17)
medicus (20)
medius (9)
melior (16)
mendāx (4)
mēnsa (2)
mercātor (2)
meus (5)
mīles (18)
minimē! (11)
mīrābilis (12)
miser (15)
mittere (12)
mōns (12)
mors (20)
mortuus (7)
mox (9)
multī (5)

multitūdō (17)
multus (5)
mūrus (11)

n
nam (18)
nārrāre (7)
nauta (15)
nāvigāre (16)
nāvis (3)
necāre (7)
necesse (14)
neglegēns (19)
negōtium (17)
negōtium agere (4)
nēmō (18)
nihil (7)
nōbilis (14)
nōlle (13)
nōn (3)
nōnne? (16)
nōs (10)
noster (11)
nōtus (9)
novem (19)
nōvisse (19)
novus (13)
nox (18)
nūbēs (12)
nūllus (13)
num? (14)
numerāre (13)
numquam (17)
nunc (11)
nūntiāre (10)
nūntius (8)

o
obstāre (18)
octō (20)
oculus (20)
offerre (9)
ōlim (6)
omnis (7)

optimē (12)
optimus (5)
ōrdō (13)
ostendere (9)

p
paene (12)
parāre (7)
parātus (16)
parēns (20)
pars (18)
parvus (6)
pater (1)
paucī (17)
paulīsper (9)
pāx (10)
pecūnia (4)
per (6)
perīculōsus (18)
perīculum (19)
perīre (16)
persuādēre (20)
perterritus (4)
pervenīre (17)
pēs (8)
pessimus (20)
pestis (7)
petere (= attack) (5)
petere (= beg for) (18)
placēre (11)
plaudere (5)
plaustrum (15)
plūrimī (19)
plūrimus (19)
pōculum (7)
poēta (4)
pompa (19)
pōnere (16)
porta (8)
portāre (3)
portus (10)
poscere (19)
posse (13)

post (9)
posteā (18)
postquam (6)
postrēmō (18)
postrīdiē (16)
postulāre (8)
praeesse (15)
praesidium (18)
precēs (20)
pretiōsus (14)
prīmus (11)
prīnceps (15)
prior (15)
prō (18)
prōcēdere (7)
prōcumbere (18)
prōmittere (11)
prope (7)
puella (5)
puer (8)
pugna (11)
pugnāre (8)
pulcher (7)
pulsāre (6)
pūnīre (15)

q
quadrāgintā (20)
quaerere (4)
quam (= how) (14)
quam (= than) (10)
quamquam (14)
quattuor (20)
-que (14)
quī (15)
quīnquāgintā (20)
quīnque (20)
quis? (4)
quō? (18)
quod (6)
quondam (17)
quoque (2)

r
rapere (11)
recipere (17)
recumbere (8)
recūsāre (18)
reddere (4)
redīre (15)
relinquere (20)
remedium (20)
rēs (6)
resistere (18)
respondēre (3)
retinēre (13)
revenīre (9)
rēx (14)
rīdēre (3)
rogāre (7)
ruere (13)

s
sacer (18)
sacerdōs (15)
saepe (8)
saevīre (18)
saltāre (16)
salūtāre (2)
salvē! (3)
sanguis (8)
satis (4)
saxum (15)
scrībere (6)
sē (13)
secundus (11)
sed (4)
sedēre (1)
sella (14)
semper (10)
senātor (11)
senex (5)
sententia (10)
sentīre (12)
septem (20)
sermō (20)
servāre (10)

Cumulated List of Checklist Words

servus (1)
sex (20)
sīcut (20)
signum (4)
silva (8)
simulac (16)
sine (17)
solēre (17)
sollicitus (11)
sōlus (10)
sonitus (19)
sordidus (17)
spectāculum (8)
spectāre (5)
stāre (5)
statim (8)
stola (19)
stultus (11)
suāviter (13)
subitō (6)
summus (16)
superāre (6)
superesse (16)
surgere (3)
suus (9)

t
taberna (3)
tacēre (10)
tacitē (7)
tam (20)

tamen (7)
tandem (12)
templum (12)
temptāre (20)
tenēre (15)
tergum (17)
terra (12)
terrēre (7)
tertius (11)
timēre (12)
tollere (16)
tot (19)
tōtus (8)
trādere (9)
trahere (13)
trēs (12 & 20)
trīgintā (20)
tū (4)
tuba (8)
tum (6)
turba (5)
tuus (6)

u
ubi (= when) (14)
ubi (= where) (5)
umbra (7)
umerus (19)
unda (15)
ūnus (12 & 20)
urbs (5)

ūtilis (11)
uxor (10)

v
valdē (17)
valē! (11)
vehementer (10)
velle (13)
vēnātiō (8)
vēndere (4)
venīre (5)
verberāre (11)
vertere (16)
vexāre (19)
via (1)
victor (15)
vidēre (3)
vīgintī (20)
vīlla (3)
vincere (15)
vīnum (3)
vir (11)
vīta (17)
vituperāre (6)
vīvere (19)
vix (19)
vocāre (4)
vōs (10)
vōx (19)
vulnerāre (13)
vulnus (20)

Appendix B: Summary of Changes from the North American Second Edition

General

The principles on which the North American Second Edition was designed remain the same for this Edition (see "Objectives of the Course," in the Unit 1 Teacher's Manual, pp. 5–6), and the North American Third Edition is compatible with the North American Second Edition. In the Third Edition, however, the students' textbook has been written in American English throughout, with punctuation, spelling, and analogies in the American style; many new photographs, including color ones, have been added; several new drawings have been prepared specifically for this Edition (notably those on p. 50 (apotheosis of Claudius' effigy), p. 88 (arrival of Rok bird at nest of jewels), and p. 109 (sacred cat attacking Eutychus)).

Changes from the North American Second Edition of Units IIA and IIB include the following:

1 Units IIA and IIB, with the accompanying Language Information pamphlets, have been combined into one Unit, now called Unit 2, with an Arabic numeral to avoid confusion between the name of the textbook and "Latin II," the traditional name for second-year high-school Latin. In most high schools, Unit 2 will be used during the second half of Latin I, the first year of Latin or, in junior high schools, in the 8th grade.

2 The students' material in Units IIA and IIB has been bound, with the two former Language Information pamphlets, into a single hardbound volume. There have been added a new Reference Grammar, which will provide students with an overview of forms and syntax; an Index of Cultural Topics (formerly in the Units IIA/IIB Teacher's Manual, p. 89); a new Index of Grammatical Topics; and a new Time Chart.

3 The contents of the two former Language Information pamphlets have been collated into a single Language Information Section. Part One of the Language Information Section has had its name changed from "About the language" to "Review Grammar"; the former Part Two, or the "Words and phrases" part, has been renamed the "Complete Vocabulary" and transferred to Part Three, thus making room for the new "Reference Grammar," which now becomes Part Two. The

"Guides to Characters and Places" from the two former Language Information pamphlets have been collated into a single Guide but still appear, as previously, immediately after the Complete Vocabulary.

4 Latin Names and Proper Adjectives are now glossed in sections separate from the other Latin words in the running vocabularies.

5 In the Background Material of Stage 18 in the students' textbook, the sub-section entitled "Glassmaking" (pp. 112–14) has been completely rewritten to incorporate the most recent scholarship on the history of Roman glassmaking, as has the commentary on glassmaking in the Unit 2 Teacher's Manual, pp. 71–73. In the Background Material of Stage 20 in the students' textbook, the diagram illustrating Eratosthenes' method of calculating the circumference of the earth has been redrawn to make it clearer, and new diagrams illustrating the workings of Ctesibius' pump and water organ have been added. In the Introduction to the Unit 2 Teacher's Manual, the section on Alexandria, called the "Cultural Importance of Roman Alexandria (Stages 17–20)," pp. 6–11, has been expanded to include commentary on the photographs of modern Alexandria which have been added to the students' textbook (notably p. 85 (Pompey's Pillar), p. 92 (Fort of Kait Bey), p. 93 (aerial view of the modern Double Harbor), and p. 101 (Roman Theater)) and complemented with a map of modern Alexandria marked with the locations of ancient sites within the city.

6 A new drill, called Word Search, follows the Words and Phrases Checklist in every Stage. This drill uses Latin words in the preceding checklist as clues for matching definitions with the correct English words.

7 The Teacher's Manual has been streamlined to make it more accessible. New charts outlining Narrative Points, Grammatical Points, and Sentence Patterns have been introduced into the beginning of each of the Stage Commentaries. The Bibliography has been updated. As there is now a Word Search drill in every Stage of the students' textbook, the lists of derivatives formerly in Appendix A of the Units IIA/IIB Teacher's Manual have been omitted.

Bibliography

Books marked with an asterisk (*) are suitable for use by junior high or high school students; other books, by college or university students (or high school students under the teacher's guidance). Included are some recommended books which, though out of print (O.P.), may sometimes be found in libraries or second-hand bookstores.

Unless stated otherwise, publishers cited are British. But if a book printed in Great Britain is or was available from a North American distributor, the name of the latter—should it differ from that of the British publisher—is listed. If in print, British books without North American distributors may be ordered from Heffers Bookstore, 10 Trinity Street, Cambridge CB2 3NG, England. To establish a personal account (and obtain instructions for ordering), request an application blank from Heffers, c/o Customers' Accounts Department, P.O. Box 33, Cambridge CB2 1TX, England.

For up-to-date listings of audio-visual materials, consult the annual listings in *Classical World*: the most recent is J.C. Traupman, "1987 Survey of Audio-Visual Materials in the Classics," *Classical World* Vol. 80, 1987, pp. 245–309.

For a current list of supplementary materials and examinations available specifically for users of the *Cambridge Latin Course*, write to William D. Gleason, Director, Resource Center, North American Cambridge Classics Project (NACCP), Box 932, Amherst, MA 01004-0932, U.S.A.

Books for Stages 13–16: Roman Britain

Cultural Background

Andrews, I. **Boudica Against Rome* (formerly *Boudicca's Revolt*) (Cambridge U.P. 1972)
Balsdon, J.P.V.D. *Life and Leisure in Ancient Rome* (Bodley Head 1969 O.P.)
Barrett, A.A. "The Career of Tiberius Claudius Cogidubnus," *Britannia* X (1979) 227–42
Birley, A.R. *Life in Roman Britain* (Batsford rev. edn 1976; North Pomfret, VT: David and Charles)
Bogaers, J.E. "King Cogidubnus in Chichester: Another Reading of *RIB* 91," *Britannia* X (1979) 243–54

Burn, A.R. (ed.) *The Romans in Britain: an anthology of inscriptions* (Blackwell 1967 O.P.)
Cambridge School Classics Project. *The Romans discover Britain* and *Teacher's Handbook* (Cambridge U.P. 1981)
Clayton, P.A. (ed.) *A Companion to Roman Britain* (Phaidon 1980; New York City, NY: State Mutual Book, O.P.) Contains useful "Gazetteer" of all sites of Roman Britain.
Collingwood, R.G. and Richmond, I.A. *The Archaeology of Roman Britain* (Methuen rev. edn 1969)
Cottrell, L. *The Great Invasion* (Evans 1958 O.P.)
Seeing Roman Britain (Pan rev. edn 1967 O.P.)
Cunliffe, B. *Excavations at Fishbourne 1961–69* (Society of Antiquaries 1971)
Fishbourne: a Roman Palace and its Garden (Thames and Hudson 1971; Baltimore, MD: Johns Hopkins, O.P.)
The Iron Age Communities in Britain (Routledge 1978)
The Regni (Peoples of Roman Britain Series: Duckworth 1973; Atlantic Highlands, NJ: Humanities Press, O.P.)
Doncaster, I. and Bullard, I. *The Roman Occupation of Britain* (Evidence in Pictures Series: Longman 1961 O.P.)
Dudley, D.R. and Webster, G. *The Rebellion of Boudicca* (Routledge 1962)
Durant, G. *Britain, Rome's Most Northerly Province* (Bell 1969 O.P.)
Fox, Lady A. and Sorrell, A. *Roman Britain* (Lutterworth Press 1961)
Frayn, J.M. *Sheep-Rearing and the Wool Trade in Italy during the Roman Period* (Francis Cairns 1984)
Frere, S.S. *Britannia: a History of Roman Britain* (Routledge rev. edn 1978)
Green, M. *Roman Technology and Crafts* (Aspects of Roman Life Series: Longman 1979)
Harvey, L.A. and J.A. *The Roman Engineers* (Cambridge U.P. 1981)
Jashemski, W.F. *The Gardens of Pompeii, Herculaneum and the Villas Destroyed by Vesuvius* (New Rochelle, NY: Caratzas Brothers 1979) For comparisons with Fishbourne garden.
Jennison, G. *Animals for Show and Pleasure in Ancient Rome* (Manchester U.P. 1937 O.P.)
Jones, D. and P. *The Villas of Roman Britain* (Jackdaw: Cape 1973 O.P.)
Jones, E.H., Jones, B. and Hayhoe, M. (eds.) *Roman Britain* ("Themes" Series, pbd: Routledge 1972) Recommended. An anthology of sources in translation, poetry and extracts from historical novels.
Liversidge, J. *Britain in the Roman Empire* (Routledge 1968)
Furniture in Roman Britain (Academy Editions 1973 O.P.)
Roman Britain ("Then and There" Series: Longman 1968)
Margary, I.D. *Roman Roads in Britain* (Baker 3rd edn 1973)
Neuberger, A. *The Technical Arts and Sciences of the Ancients*, tr. H.L. Brose (Methuen Library Reprints 1969 O.P.)

Bibliography

Percival, J. *The Roman Villa* (Batsford 1976; Berkeley, CA: University of California Press)
Priestley, H.E. *Britain under the Romans* (Warne 1967 O.P.)
Richmond, Sir I.A. *Roman Britain* (Pelican new issue 1970)
Rivet, A.L.F. *The Roman Villa in Britain* (Studies in Ancient History and Archaeology: Routledge 1969)
 Town and Country in Roman Britain (Hutchinson 1966)
Rule, M. *Fishbourne Roman Palace Guide* (Sussex Archaeological Society 1977)
 Floor Mosaics in Roman Britain (Macmillan 1974 O.P.)
Ryder, M.L. "The Evolution of the Fleece," *Scientific American* CCLVI (January 1987) 112–119
Salway, P. *Roman Britain* (Oxford History of England, Vol. IA: Oxford U.P. 1981)
Scullard, H.H., *Roman Britain: Outpost of the Empire* (Thames & Hudson 1979)
Sellmann, R.R.S. *Roman Britain* (Methuen 3rd edn 1964 O.P.)
Sorrell, A. *Roman Towns in Britain* (Batsford 1976; North Pomfret, VT: David and Charles, O.P.)
Strong, D. and Brown, D. (eds.) *Roman Crafts* (Duckworth 1976; New York City, NY: Columbia U.P.)
Susini, G. *The Roman Stonecutter* (Totowa, NJ: Littlefield, Adams and Co. 1973, O.P.)
Tingay, G. *From Caesar to the Saxons* (Longman 1969)
Toynbee, J.M.C. *Animals in Roman Life and Art* (Aspects of Greek and Roman Life Series: Ithaca, NY: Cornell U.P. 1973)
Wacher, J. *Roman Britain* (Dent 1978; Totowa, NJ: Biblio Distribution Center)
Webster, G. *Boudica: British Revolt against Rome A.D. 60* (Batsford 1978; Totowa, NJ: Rowman & Littlefield Inc., O.P.)
 The Roman Invasion of Britain (Batsford 1980; Totowa, NJ: Littlefield, Adams and Co., O.P.)
 Rome against Caratacus: the Roman Campaigns in Britain A.D. 48–58 (Batsford 1981; Totowa, NJ: Littlefield, Adams and Co., O.P.)
Webster, G. and Dudley, D.R. *The Roman Conquest of Britain A.D. 43–57* (British Battles Series: Batsford 1966 O.P.)
White, K.D. *Roman Farming* (Ithaca, NY: Cornell U.P. 1970, O.P.)
Wilson, R.J.A. *Guide to the Roman Remains in Britain* (Constable 2nd edn 1980; New York City, NY: State Mutual Book, O.P.)

Source Material for the Roman World Generally

Apicius. *The Roman Cookery Book*, trs. B. Flower and E. Rosenbaum (Harrap 1974)

Cambridge School Classics Project. **The Roman World* Units I and II (Cambridge U.P. 1978–9)
Lewis, N. and Reinhold, M. *Roman Civilization: a Sourcebook—I The Republic*; *II The Empire* (Harper Torchbooks: Harper and Row 1966)
Pliny. **Letters*: a selection, tr. C. Greig (Cambridge U.P. 1978)

Reference

C.I.L. *Corpus Inscriptionum Latinarum* (Berlin, 1863–)
Dessau, H. *Inscriptiones Latinae Selectae* (Berlin, 1892–1916)
R.I.B. Collingwood, R.G. and Wright, R.P., *The Roman Inscriptions of Britain* (Oxford U.P. 1965)

Historical Novels

Duggan, A. **The Little Emperors* (Faber 1951 O.P.)
Kipling, R. **Puck of Pook's Hill* (Macmillan 1951; Piccolo 1975)
Marris, R. **The Cornerstone* ("Long Ago" Series: Heinemann 1976) A story about the son of a Fishbourne mosaicist.
Plowman, S. **To Spare the Conquered* (Methuen 1960 O.P.) Set at the time of the conquest of Britain and Boudica's revolt.
Ray, M. **The Eastern Beacon* (New York City, NY: Farrar, Straus and Giroux 1965, O.P.) The adventures of a young Greek girl and Roman boy who are shipwrecked on the Scilly Isles in the 3rd century A.D.
    *Spring Tide (Faber pbd 1979; Winchester, MA: Faber and Faber, Inc.) Two boys encounter Christianity for the first time.
Seton, A. **The Mistletoe and The Sword* (Brockhampton 1956 O.P.) Set at the time of Boudica's revolt.
Sutcliff, R. **The Eagle of the Ninth* (Oxford U.P. 1954; Puffin 1977) A young Roman officer tries to recover the lost eagle of the vanished Ninth Legion. Perhaps the best of its kind.
    *The Silver Branch (Oxford U.P. 1957; Puffin 1980) Sequel to the above, set 170 years later.
    *The Lantern Bearers (Oxford U.P. 1972) A Roman soldier remains after the withdrawal from Britain and helps to fight the invading Saxons.
    *Outcast (Oxford U.P. 1955) A young British tribesman is sold into slavery.
Treece, H. **Legions of the Eagle* (Bodley Head 1954; Puffin 1965) The story of a boy living during the invasion of A.D. 43.
    *War Dog (Brockhampton 1962 O.P.) A story about Bran, the huge war dog of Caratacus' charioteer.
    *The Queen's Brooch (Hamilton 1966 O.P.) The life of a young Roman who encounters Boudica.

Wheeler, M. *The Farthermost Fort* (Dent 1969 O.P.) This story centers on the final withdrawal of the Romans from Britain.

Books for Stages 17–20: Alexandria

Cultural Background

Cambridge Ancient History, Vol. XI (Cambridge U.P. 1936)
Cambridge School Classics Project. **Pompey and Caesar* and *Teacher's Handbook* (Cambridge U.P. 1986) **The Romans discover Britain* and *Teacher's Handbook* (Cambridge U.P. 1981)
 **The Roman World* Units I and II (Cambridge U.P. 1978–9)
Lewis, N. and Reinhold, M. *Roman Civilization: a Sourcebook, Vol. II The Empire* (Harper Torchbooks, Harper and Row 1966)
McEvedy, C. **Penguin Atlas of Ancient History* (Penguin 1970)
Paoli, U.E. *Rome, its People, Life and Customs* (Westport, CT: Greenwood Press 1964, O.P.)

Literary Influence

Cavafy, C.P. *The Complete Poems of Cavafy*, expanded edn, tr. Rae Dalven, with Introduction by W.H. Auden (New York: Harcourt Brace Jovanovich 1976)
 Collected Poems, tr. E. Keeley and P. Sherrard, ed. G. Savidis (Princeton U.P. 1975)
Forster, E.M. *Pharos and Pharillon*, 3rd edn (Hogarth 1961; Berkeley, CA: Creative Arts Books)
Keeley, E. *Cavafy's Alexandria: Study of a Myth in Progress* (Cambridge, MA: Harvard U.P. 1976)

History; Trade

Badian, E. *"Ancient Alexandria," *History Today* 10, November 1960
Evans, I.O. **Gadget City: A Story of Ancient Alexandria* (Warne 1944 O.P.) Novel about a Welsh slave captured in Britain and sent to work at the Museum in Alexandria.
Forster, E.M. **Alexandria: A History and Guide*, 2nd edn by M. von Haag (M. Haag 1981; New York City, NY: Oxford U.P. 1986)
Fraser, P.M. *Ptolemaic Alexandria*, 3 vols. (Oxford U.P. 1972; rprt 1984)
Hodge, P. **Roman Trade and Travel* (Longman 1978)
Lindsay, J. *Daily Life in Roman Egypt* (Muller 1963 O.P.)
 Leisure and Pleasure in Roman Egypt (Muller 1965 O.P.)
Marlowe, J. **The Golden Age of Alexandria* (Gollancz 1971 O.P.)
Meiggs, R. *Roman Ostia* (Oxford U.P. 2nd edn 1974 O.P.)

Severin, Tim. *The Sindbad Voyage* (Hutchinson 1982) Recreation of a medieval Arab trader's voyage, the historical basis of Sindbad's legendary adventures.
Thorley, J. "The Silk Trade between China and the Roman Empire at its Height, circa A.D. 90–130," *Greece and Rome* N.S. 18, April 1971

Roman-Egyptian Religion

Apuleius. *The Golden Ass,* tr. R. Graves (Penguin Classics 1972)
Griffiths, J. Gwyn. *The Isis-Book* (Apuleius, *Metamorphoses* XI) (Brill 1975)
Lindsay, J. *Men and Gods on the Roman Nile* (Muller 1968 O.P.)
  Origins of Astrology (Muller 1970 O.P.)
Solmsen, Friedrich. *Isis among the Greeks and Romans* (Cambridge, MA: Harvard U.P. 1980, O.P.)
Witt, R.E. *Isis in the Graeco-Roman World* (Aspects of Greek and Roman Life Series: Ithaca, NY: Cornell U.P. 1971, O.P.)

Greek and Roman Medicine, Science, and Technology

Boston Museum of Fine Arts. *Ancient Glass in the Museum of Fine Arts* (1968)
Clagett, M. *Greek Science in Antiquity* (Salem, N.H.: Ayer Company Publishers 1955)
Davies, R.W. "Medicine in Ancient Rome," *History Today* 21, November 1971
Farrington, B. *Greek Science: Its Meaning for Us* (Spokesman Books 1981)
Green, M. *Roman Technology and Crafts* (Aspects of Roman Life Series: Longman 1979)
Hamey, L.A. and J.A. *The Roman Engineers* (Cambridge U.P. 1981; Minneapolis, MN: Lerner Publications)
Harden, D.B. *Ancient Glass II: Roman.* Reprint from *The Archaeological Journal* Vol. CXXVI (1969) (available from Royal Archaeological Institute, c/o Addison House, Grove End Rd, London NW8 9EL)
Heuer, K. *City of the Stargazers* (New York: Charles Scribner's Sons 1972 O.P.)
Hodges, H. *Technology in the Ancient World* (New York City, NY: Random House 1970)
Hull, L.W.H. *History and Philosophy of Science* (Longman 1959 O.P.)
Kingery, W.D. and Lense, E. (eds.) *Ceramics and Civilization – III: High-Technology Ceramics* (Westerville, OH: The American Ceramic Society, Inc. 1986)
Klein, D. and Lloyd, W. (eds.) *The History of Glass* (London: Orbis 1984)

Landels, J. *Engineering in the Ancient World* (Chatto and Windus 1978; Berkeley, CA: University of California Press)

Lee, Sir D. "Science, Philosophy and Technology in the Greco-Roman World," *Greece and Rome* N.S. 20, April, October 1973

Lewis, N. *Life in Egypt under Roman Rule* (Oxford U.P. 1983)

Majno, G. *The Healing Hand: Man and Wound in the Ancient World* (Cambridge, MA: Harvard U.P. 1975)

Sarton, G. *A History of Science, Vol. II Hellenistic Science and Culture in the Last Three Centuries B.C.* (Cambridge, MA: Harvard U.P. 1959 O.P.)

Scarborough, J. *Roman Medicine* (Aspects of Greek and Roman Life Series: Ithaca, NY: Cornell U.P. 1969, O.P.)

Singer, C. *Greek Biology and Greek Medicine* (New York City, NY: AMS Press 1922)

Stahl, W.H. *Roman Science: Origins, Development and Influence to the Later Middle Ages* (Westport, CT: Greenwood Press 1962; rprt 1978)

Strong, D. and Brown, D. (eds.) *Roman Crafts* (Duckworth 1976; New York City, NY: Columbia U.P.)

Taton, R. (ed.). *History of Science: Ancient and Medieval Science from the Beginnings to 1450*, tr. A.J. Pomerans (New York City: Basic Books 1963 O.P.)